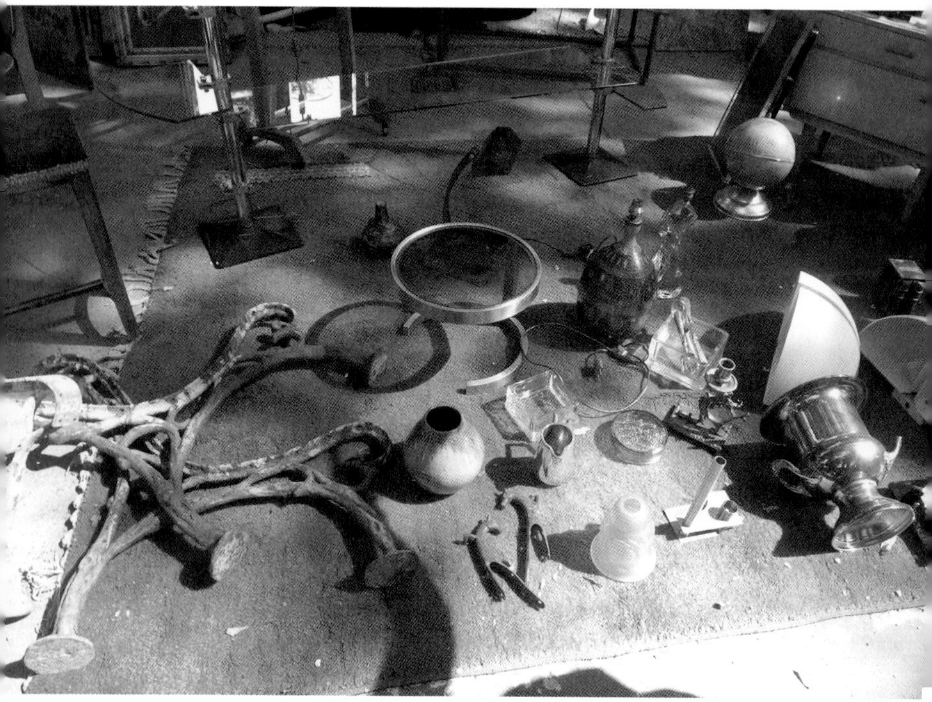

Fleamarket at the Porte de Vanves, July 2010
Detail of *From Margin to Margin (Looking for Eileen)*, 2010
46 page folding leperello, 7360mm when fully extended,
edition of 200. Commissioned by the Daimler Art Collection
Proceeds from the sale of the book to be used in the service of
the memory of Eileen Gray

Foreword

Sarah Browne's practice addresses 'the economy' as the overriding metaphor for contemporary social and political relations. Within the current global economic climate and ongoing debate of cutbacks, austerity measures and failing markets, her artistic practice could not be more relevant. She is concerned in working with or documenting small-scale constituencies that establish intentional economies or temporary 'communities', the work often carried out with the participation of such a grouping or by creating a fictional network within the logic of the work itself. Through these structures, types of non-market exchange such as gift economies, subsistence, subsidies and poaching tend to form, often as a summation of collective intention or desire, typically influenced by emotional affects. By processes such as filmmaking, sculpture and publishing the potential for a more radical resourcefulness is sought as a manifestation of creative opposition to prevailing systems.

How to Use Fool's Gold, the title of the exhibition and this book, hints at impulses of desire and desperation, the less rational drives that may underpin large-scale economic movements. Otherwise known as pyrite, 'fool's gold' is a crystalline mineral with a lustrous metallic appearance, often mistaken for gold while prospecting. Such concerns in relation to material resources, and the poetic-pragmatic attempt to fashion something out of nothing, manifest in different ways in Browne's work. Thought-to-be-useless materials and objects are repurposed, such as the apparently disappointing fool's gold finding a use as a detector in a functioning crystal radio, enabling the reception of radio signal without any electrical input at all. Extracts of texts are presented and collated as specific interventions, or performative excavations, as a way of mining, a retrieving of overlooked or alternative value or knowledge. Writing and publishing plays an increasingly significant part of her artistic production, seen in text-based artworks and the reproduced essays herein, her editorial role important as a crucial part of her essential *modus operandi*. By extension such strategies themselves can be seen as suggestive of the idea of the art object itself, and its uncertain value, or surprising potential, as a kind of fool's gold.

Central to the three exhibitions is a newly co-commissioned work *Second Burial at Le Blanc* (2011). For its first incarnation in Dublin it comprised a looped 16mm colour film alongside a ticker-tape countdownclock with customised printer, all housed in a glass dome on a wooden plinth. Filmed in the small French town which gives the work its title, it follows a procession in which residents carry the machine through city streets, from the old town to the new. What is central to the piece is that the town exists outside of the mainstream, still trading internally with the franc in exchange for goods and services, and able to do so until February 17, 2012 when the Central Bank of France will no longer replace the currency for euros. As the film unfolds, the commemorative nature of the event, as we head toward the date of redundancy for the old currency, seems ever more poignant, a sort of anti-monument in progress to what Le Blanc represents as a working alternative to the current state of affairs across Europe and the world.

Other projects surround the core gallery presentations. For Birmingham Browne has developed *Scarcity Radio* in order to investigate our understanding of scarcity in the current economic context, focusing particularly on the role of radio communication during moments of social crisis. In collaboration with Ikon's youth programme, IYP, a set of film-screenings, discussions and workshops examine the culture of pirate radio in the 1980s, a previous moment of major recession, in relation to what may be urgent today. The knowledge produced informs the 'reception and broadcast' of a summer programme from on board a narrow boat navigating the canals in and around this sprawling inland city.

In Dublin an accompanying performative reading linking Project Arts Centre to the Geology Museum of Trinity College took place, between the artist Jesse Jones and Sarah Browne. Leading participants through a reading of Sahlins' *Stone Age Economics*, ideas and themes of economic ritual, invented tradition and obsolescence were explored by the group, as they wandered through the Geology collection, past Ireland's Central Bank, and returned to Project Arts Centre. The event and readings titled *The Original Affluent Society*, reproduced here, proposed a re-visioning of hunter-gatherer societies from being 'primitive' to seeing them as practitioners of a refined mode of subsistence, from which much can be learned.

This collaboration between all three institutions marks a significant development for Browne allowing for an expansion of her practice through the exhibition and associated publication, and their reception worldwide. That *Second Burial at Le Blanc* evolves in differing forms across all three exhibitions retains an appropriate sense of local economy and opportunity within the bigger picture of shared possibilities. Starting in Dublin in May 2011 at a time of Irish monetary insecurity could not have been more appropriate. Within this context we are extremely grateful for major help from key supporters. The Arts Council / An Chomhairle Ealaíon have played a crucial role in granting funds toward the production of *Second Burial at Le Blanc*; likewise Culture Ireland has been key in generating considerable resources to enable us to achieve this overall project – a vital investment in a young artist at an important stage of her career.

We take this opportunity to thank Jeremy Millar for his insightful essay, the anthropological and ethnographic interests within his own practice chiming perfectly with those of Browne. Likewise we are indebted to writers

Dr. Marshall Sahlins and Chris Lee and their respective publishers for permission to reprint existing texts; that Chris Lee took the opportunity to revise his for this context is particularly exciting. We also thank Lucina Russell and Kildare County Council for the loan of the *Carpet for the Irish Pavilion at the Venice Biennale* from their municipal collection for the two exhibitions in Birmingham and Vancouver, allowing for audiences a larger overview of Browne's practice.

And so to Sarah Browne, an artist of great thoughtfulness, precision and quiet passion, we thank her for her energy and enthusiasm, and for her unstinting attention to the various aspects and opportunities present within the context of each exhibition. That she approached each venue as a discrete but inter-related project, keen to develop new ideas pertinent to each place, underscores the relevance of her artistic proposition asking us to consider again local factors within a broader global confluence. She could not have been better company on this journey.

Tessa Giblin
Curator of Visual Arts, Project Arts Centre, Dublin

Nigel Prince
Executive Director, Contemporary Art Gallery, Vancouver

Jonathan Watkins
Director, Ikon Gallery, Birmingham

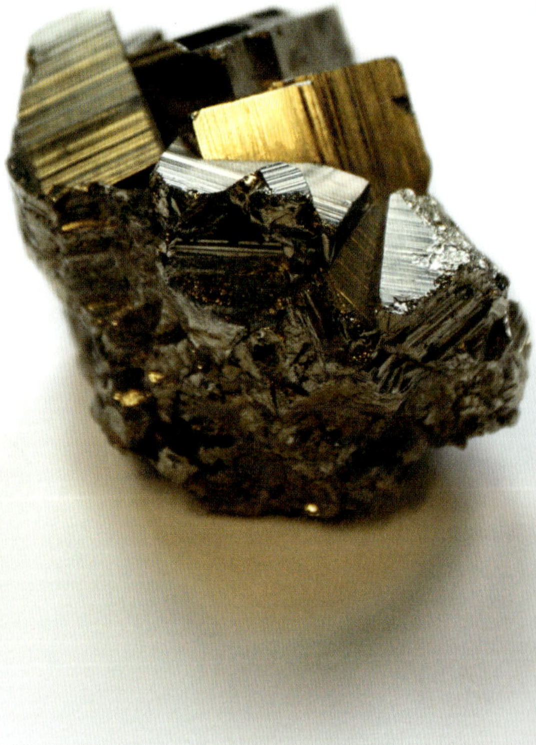

How to Use Fool's Gold (Pyrite Radio), production detail, 2012
Dimensions variable

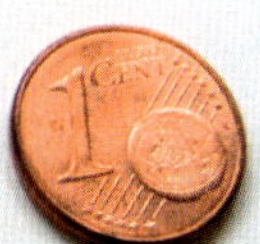
1 CENT

Making Objects That Make Talk

Jeremy Millar

> "All of us who sit down in front of a computer keyboard know that we find out what we think about things by reading what we are writing."
>
> —Bruno Latour

If making art is a strange and somewhat mysterious process, then writing about it is seldom simpler. Even looking at it (even looking!) is fraught with difficulties, as what one sees most often depends upon what it is one is looking for. Although these lines are (probably) where you are beginning the reading of this essay, it is where I am coming to my end, as the last lines I will here write. It is only now that I know what follows, looking back over what, for you, is yet to come, and what has emerged (will emerge) is not quite what I had anticipated. ('Planned' seems too definitive a term.) I had thought to write a piece both shorter, and more extensive, than this now is, one that made reference to the great diversity of Sarah Browne's practice, in both form and subject matter, from elegant door-stoppers to rather folksy knitted jumpers, and in this my thoughts coincided with those of others. Certain means were established, materials gathered, questions asked; photocopied margins were marked in halting red lines and books fringed with plastic page markers; piles were made, and then scattered, and brought together once more, of the same things (mostly) although now is a different order. I had thought to write about the economy within Browne's work, the 'accursed share' of its expenditure, and yet now, having re-read the relevant books, as well as the more recent commentaries, I now found that this is not what I have written

at all, although it is difficult to characterise this, now, as a waste of time and energy. (And in any case, wouldn't that be a good thing in such a context?) No, instead I find reading now that I have written about only one of Browne's works, *How to Make Muscha in Vaasa* (2010), which was developed during a residency in September and October 2009 at Platform, in Vaasa, on the western coast of Finland. In keeping with many other similar artists' initiatives, Platform's projects often emphasise the importance of locality and the specifics of place, encouraging visiting artists to work with those native to or at least resident in, the town. In developing this work, Browne sensitively brought some of her own interests, and native concerns, to bear upon those she found while in Vaasa, allowing different forms of 'local' knowledge to come into communication with one another, or, perhaps better, to act together.

The 'muscha' that was to be made in Vaasa is 'a flavourless and odourless spirit', the word from the Swedish-Finnish dialect for 'moonshine', the term returning to the region with those who had previously emigrated to the US (although it was in production far earlier than this). Although Browne had intended to make a film that used alcoholic intoxication (and the inevitable hangover) as a metaphor for the euphoria of economic boom (and painful slump), her interest settled instead upon the *actual making* of muscha, and how this was dependent upon a particular economy of its own. The making of illicit alcohol is not unique to this region, of course, and Browne was well aware of the production of *poitín* back in Ireland (when she lived in the north-west, there was always someone who had a source of good *poitín*, or knew someone who did). Indeed, it was perhaps the very ubiquity of this fermenting of sugar and water with local starches, not just in northern Europe but around the world, that suggested its production as a suitable subject for cultural comparison: if the product is the same, so much better to highlight the differences of that which surrounds it.

Although its title suggests a set of simple instructions, *How to Make Muscha in Vaasa* is a rather more complex work than first meets the eye; indeed, we must decide as to what it is, exactly, that meets the eye, what it is that we are looking at. Perhaps the most important thing is something to read, rather than more simply look at, the text that is laid across seven A5 pages, and then spread across the gallery wall. (It is also reproduced in this publication.) Given the omnipresence of such illicit distillation, and that the project could be similarly repeated in other places, Browne established the basic format on the first page: the title (a variation upon 'How to make *X* in *Y*', where *X* is the local name for the spirit, and *Y* is the place of its production); a simple description; and six instructions, each with an explanatory endnote on a subsequent, and separate, page. Although the simple re-iterative nature of this opening text suggests some of the instructions to be found within works from the classic period of Conceptual Art, the comments in the endnotes that follow possess a quite different character. If the initial instructions consisted of verbs and their objects, here the subject appears, the first-person-singular who, with others, talks and travels, buys and builds. If Browne's practice could be considered a form of anthropological enquiry, then here her role was that of the participant-observer, and rather more participant than observer, not only searching out the means by which the spirit might be produced, but then going on to obtain them, and to putting them to use, also. This is the other fantasy of the anthropologist, the fantasy-other, the elimination of distance, of initiation, even, as a means of coming to a greater understanding of what it is one is studying, even of becoming what one is studying. Such is the position that French ethnographer Michel Leiris began to seek towards the end of participation in the Dakar–Djibouti Mission in 1931–33: "Intense work, to which I give myself with a certain assiduousness, but without an ounce of passion. I'd rather be possessed than study possessed people, have carnal knowledge of a *zarine*, rather than know all about her. For me, abstract knowledge will never be anything but a second best."[1]

If we read her endnotes, however, there was no simple co-incidence for Browne, and for all her best intentions (if such they were) it was difficult to 'go native' completely. The difficulties (for an English-speaker) of the Finnish and Swedish languages—Vaasa, beside the Gulf of Ostrobothnia, is home to both—were a fundamental obstacle, and a number of different people were required to translate recipes, packaging labels, and instructions. ('Secure collaborators' is the first instruction, yet it might just as well be a description of one of the more important qualities required of them.) Through the efforts of her collaborators, however, a degree of trust was established, and it is interesting that the most obvious transitional point within the text comes when the older shopkeeper, from whom Browne has been purchasing equipment for the still, speaks, unexpectedly, in English: "We know what you are doing you know!" In becoming, temporarily, more English he allows Browne, temporarily, to become more Finnish.[2]

Let us return to the gallery, however, wherever it is that we might find ourselves and this work, and let us ask ourselves once again: what is the work? We've glanced at the objects upon the plinth and the shelf, and turned to the text, and diagrams, on the wall nearby in search of some sort of explanation; from here we return to the objects, by now better equipped to set up the apparatus (and least mentally), to imagine its workings, and to establish the proof of its outcome. We are at a loss, however; the circuit is broken; things don't connect. Even if we believe the accuracy of the descriptions in the text, believe that this old milk churn is the still that it describes being made, and that this bottle of clear liquid, 'flavourless and odourless' also, is what the still produced in turn, even if we believe all of these things to be true, then what is the status of the things we see before us? Is this the art, or rather the means by which it came about?

Like the collaborators listed near the beginning of the accompanying text, these objects are certainly implicated in what had occurred, no matter what that might be. When Dragos, the artist who uses the studio next door, asks Browne if they can keep the still when she has finished with it, she replies no, and that she'll "have to have it to exhibit as a piece of work." Although the language Browne uses is familiar, indeed somewhat commonplace, its ambiguity is telling, or rather, the ambiguity obscures the telling. Dragos is not told that the cooking kit *is* the art (and in asking for it one suspects that Dragos thinks this not the case, either) but rather that it is a 'piece of work', a part of something that is useful, or can be made so, that is active, or can be made so; that can be made to make, and the thing that it can be made to make is art, even as it also makes something else.

It might seem rather unhelpful to make an even larger leap, in time if not in space, to help us understand what might have happened here, but in considering this work, perhaps we are not so far from the considerations of those involved in 'ethnographic surrealism' in Paris in the late 1920s and early 1930s. (Browne has also acknowledged the influence that this work has had upon her practice.) According to the historian Denis Hollier, it was a "critique of the commodity that was... to serve as the basis for the short-lived alliance between ethnographers and dissenting surrealists that was to constitute the specificity of *Documents,*" the journal co-founded, and largely edited, by numismatist, scholar, (and pornographer) Georges Bataille.[3] The journal was backed financially by the collector and dealer Georges Wildenstein, who also produced *Gazette des beaux-arts*, and with the involvement of Carl Einstein, whose pioneering *Negerplastik* (1915) considered African sculpture back through a knowledge of Cubism, one might assume that Wildenstein hoped for a journal of fine art which included the increasingly fashionable 'primitive arts' of Africa and, to a lesser extent, Oceania. Bataille, however, had rather different ideas, and the rubric he chose—'Doctrines—Archaeology—Fine Art—Ethnography'—rather declared a combination of approaches that promised little obvious compatibility with one another, a contentious coming-together of disciplines and indisciplines.[4] Even with the inclusion of 'Fine Art', the guiding ideology of the journal, under Bataille, was profoundly anti-aesthetic, or at least anti- the dominant Western aesthetics of the period. As Hollier notes, this is "signalled by the choice of the term 'ethnography' rather than the expression 'primitive arts'. It has the quality of a manifesto: it announces that *Documents* will not be another *Gazette des Beaux-Arts*, and even less a *Gazette des beaux-arts primitifs*."[5]

The writers associated with *Documents* were less interested in appreciating an object solely for its formal qualities, than for what else it might be (or might have been), or for what it might do (or have done); as such they differentiated themselves from 'amateurs', or connoisseurs, whom Leiris attacked for transforming "a mask or a statue constructed with a view to specific, complex ritual purposes into a vulgar piece of art."[6] These transformations occurred not only within the pages of contemporary art magazines, such as *Cahiers d'Art*, but also within museums and commercial galleries, some of whom even advertised within *Documents*. If the magazine's rubric had something of the manifesto, then it was one that was being enacted in the world beyond. George Henri Rivière, one of the most influential French ethnographers of the period, was both a member of the editorial board of *Documents* and deputy directory of the Musée d'Ethnographie du Trocadéro, in Paris. Under the direction of Paul Rivet, Rivière was responsible for the reorganisation of the museum, a process he wrote about in the journal's first issue; in issue 3, Rivet himself develops their thinking further, rejecting the tendency of some ethnographers to identify certain luxurious, or unusual, items as art, and so worthy of attention, while ignoring everything else that was produced in the same culture.

This impulse to look beyond the most refined could be found in many other articles within *Documents*. In his 'Critical Dictionary' definition of pottery published the following year, Marcel Griaule emphasises the use-value of the object under consideration, rather than its formal qualities, criticising those who "will admire the form of a handle," but "carefully refrain from studying the position of the man who drinks."[7] In a description that returns our attention to Browne's muscha still (previously a milk churn no less), he notes that these "archaeologists and aesthetes are interested in the container and not in the contents, in the rural scenes and the animals on the surround, and not in the milk pouring directly from the udder; in the colour of the clay and not in the smell that it could give to this milk."[8]

It is exactly these transient qualities—whether the eye-twinkling collusion of the shopkeeper, the frustration of the artist, even, appropriately, the smell of the muscha cooking in the studio—that Browne brings to our attention in the text that forms part of this work; she even acknowledges that the smell was something that she hadn't anticipated, and she draws it to our attention at the same time, it seems, as Dragos next door draws it to hers. Such qualities are emergent, and come into being through the interaction of the various elements involved, sometimes unexpectedly, and often with no great sense of certainty. They exist precariously, and so must be treated similarly, with a touch sensitive to the deathly grip of systemic thought. As Leiris, himself, expressed his concerns with regards to a monumental learning that was "in the service of those two abstractions called Art and Science," what would be "systematically excluded" was "everything that is living fermentation."[9]

Of course, 'living fermentation' is at the very heart of *Making Muscha in Vaasa*, is what helped *make* the muscha in Vaasa, and the coincidence of the term is more than just useful; it allows us to consider what it is to be useful, to be made useful, and how making, itself, is used here in this work. (Such a process is not confined to this work alone, however, and as I read this now I think of the many others in the exhibition in which it might be made similarly usefully.) In considering this work, I think we might detect a certain generosity in Browne's approach, a revealing of how it has come about: the objects are presented simply, their construction further clarified by the text that accompanies them. One diagram further sets out the workings of pipes, taps, and containers (if this is not made entirely clear in the text), while another even shows how they are to packed into their wooden transit case or, in turn, how they are to be unpacked, and the case turned into a plinth and shelf for their display. The sharing of such information is not unusual in Browne's work, and gives it a characteristic sense of munificence, but one infers that this is less a means to explain what has occurred, than an attempt for her to understand it also, and how it might have come about. For all her attentiveness to the particulars of copper piping and rubber grommets, condensers and hygrometers, there remains something of a mystery at work here, something that resists our understanding. The task is to enable it to do so.

Let us return to the last of those six instructions-to-self on the very first page of the text within this work: 'Consider a defence.' When one is about to embark, knowingly, upon an illegal act, it is indeed a sensible precaution to consider what one might say if caught, and Browne's options are reasonable, even if not necessarily adequate. I'd like to put forward another: I didn't make it. One might consider this even more inadequate, and in a strictly legal sense it no doubt is; thankfully this is not really my concern here. Rather, I'd like to consider, briefly, what it is to make something, and to make something happen. To do so, let us imagine another act of interrogation, taking place on the west coast of Africa, Guinea, in the mid-eighteenth century rather than on the west coast of Finland at the beginning of the twenty-first.[10]

There, then, Portuguese explorers and traders came across the Gold Coast natives worshipping stone, clay, and wooden idols and demanded of them whether these were made with their own hands. Of course they were, came the reply. And were these stone, clay, and wooden idols true divinities? Of course they were, otherwise we would not have made them. For the Portuguese this was a contradiction: they were either handmade or they were divine; they could not be both. It is here that the Portuguese are thought to have used the adjective *feitiço*, from the verb 'to do, make' to describe these idols, which soon came to be known as *fetishes*. The word emerges, as the objects themselves do, from a tangle of understandings and intentions, meaning form, and figuration, but also artificial and enchanted. As the French philosopher Bruno Latour notes with regard to this episode: "The two roots of the word indicate rather well the ambiguity surrounding an object that talks, that is fabricated or, to blend both meanings into a single expression, an object that provokes talk. Yes, the fetish is a 'talk-maker'."[11]

If the native believed in fetishes, then the Westerner (even one similarly adorned in amulets) believed in facts. But in Latour's analysis, the distinction is not so clear, and by way of example he refers to the experimental analyses of Louis Pasteur, one of the West's most celebrated discoverers of scientific facts, and does so, interestingly, with reference to Pasteur's experiments with the fermentation of sugar and yeast. In his notes, Pasteur remarks, with all the disinterestedness of the realist scientist, that "*whoever* judges *impartially* the results of this work and that which I will shortly publish *will recognise with me* that fermentation appears to be correlative to life and to the organisation of globules, and not to their death or putrefaction."[12] And yet, just before this, Pasteur had created the context in which such observations might be made:

All through this memoir, I have *reasoned* on the basis of the hypothesis that the yeast is organized, that it is a living organism and that its chemical action on sugar corresponds to its development and organization. If someone were to tell me that in these conclusions I am *going beyond* that which the facts prove, I would answer that it is quite true, in the sense that *the stand I am taking is in a framework of ideas* that in rigorous terms *cannot* be irrefutably demonstrated. Here is *the way I see it...*[13]

Here facts are not simply recognised as already existing in the world, but are recognised, instead, as something made in the world, the construction of habit and presupposition. As Latour so wonderfully puts it, Pasteur "asserts in one and the same breath that the ferment of lactic acid is real because he carefully set the stage on which the ferment revealed itself on its own."[14] In his laboratory, Pasteur is able, with great skill, expertise, and judgement, to create something that is then autonomous of his creation, a process in which was established a "continuity between human work and the ferment's independence", and was this not what Browne was able to do also? After leaving the studio, the apparatus now set up, Browne returns the next day to find that "the studio is filled with a sweet, sticky aroma, and the air is gurgling softly. The yeast is alive in the big swollen plastic tub; it's breathing up through the airlock." Did Browne make the muscha? No doubt the authorities would decide 'yes', but perhaps we might decide to refrain from such a decision, and like the Guineans in the face of their Portuguese inquisitors, and Pasteur in his laboratory, allow that what has been made is at once something that is more than what has been made. In an attempt better to describe such a combinatory object, Latour creates the rather inelegant term 'factish', although for our purposes, we may use a word that is rather more familiar, or seems to be, no matter how difficult it is to understand what it might actually be: art.

It is said that the more obviously one reveals the means by which the gods are invited to the initiation, the more certain it is that the divinities are present, and I believe that we might say the same for these beautifully simple, complex works of (by? with?) Sarah Browne.[15] Whether it is in the fug of a Finnish studio, a Donegal carpet factory, or the shops of a small French town, Browne carefully identifies the various elements—whether it is turbo yeast or monetary exchange rates, surplus wool or utopia—and sets them out for us, describing how they might be joined together, placed in relationships with one another, how one might flow into another, or through another, or from another, and so lead us somewhere, and with something, quite different from what we had before. It is these that will not only make up the artwork, but that will also make the artwork. It is these that will make the art work. And it is here that we began.

1 James Clifford, *The Predicament of Culture: Twentieth-Century Ethnography, Literature, and Art* (Cambridge, Mass.: Harvard University Press, 1988), p.169

2 That Browne is not, herself, English is perhaps an example of the subtle (and not-so-subtle) distinctions which can become lost, or obscured, in forms of cultural translation, its proximity to us making it here all the more apparent.

3 Denis Hollier, 'The Use-Value of the Impossible', trans. Liesl Ollman, in *October*, Vol. 60 (Spring, 1992), p.7

4 The journal's rubric was soon changed to 'Archaeology—Fine Arts—Ethnography — Miscellanies'.

5 Hollier, op. cit., p.5

6 Leiris, *Documents* 4 (September 1929), quoted in ibid., p.12

7 Griaule, *Documents* 4 (1930), quoted in Hollier, op. cit., p.8

8 Griaule, op. cit., quoted in Julia Kelly, 'Discipline and indiscipline: the ethnographies of *Documents*' in Papers of Surrealism: The Use-Value of *Documents* Issue 7 (2007), p.13, available at *www.surrealismcentre.ac.uk/.../acrobat%20files/articles/Kellypdf.pdf*

9 Leiris, 'Du musée d'ethnographie au Musée de l'Homme', in *Nouvelle revue française* 299, p.344, quoted in Clifford, op. cit., p.144

10 For this example, and many the ideas that are developed from it, I am indebted to Bruno Latour, *On the Modern Cult of the Factish Gods* (Durham and London: Duke University Press, 2010)

11 Ibid., p.4

12 Ibid., pp.17–18 (emphasis added by Latour)

13 Ibid, p.17 (emphasis added by Latour)

14 Ibid. Perhaps this dual status, of the manufactured thing and the autonomous fact, is more easily discerned in French, where 'le fait' means both 'what somebody has fabricated', and 'what nobody has fabricated'.

15 See, for example, Michael Taussig, *Defacement: Public Secrecy and the Labor of the Negative* (Stanford: Stanford University Press, 1999). One should not forget, either, that the extensive descriptions within the text are of Browne's attempt to create pure spirit, if not a Pure Spirit.

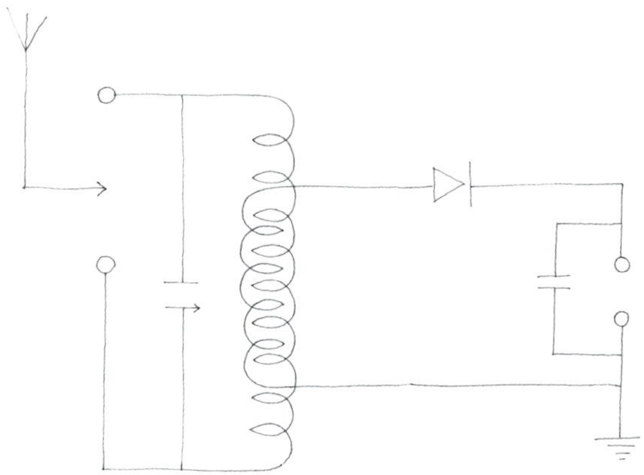

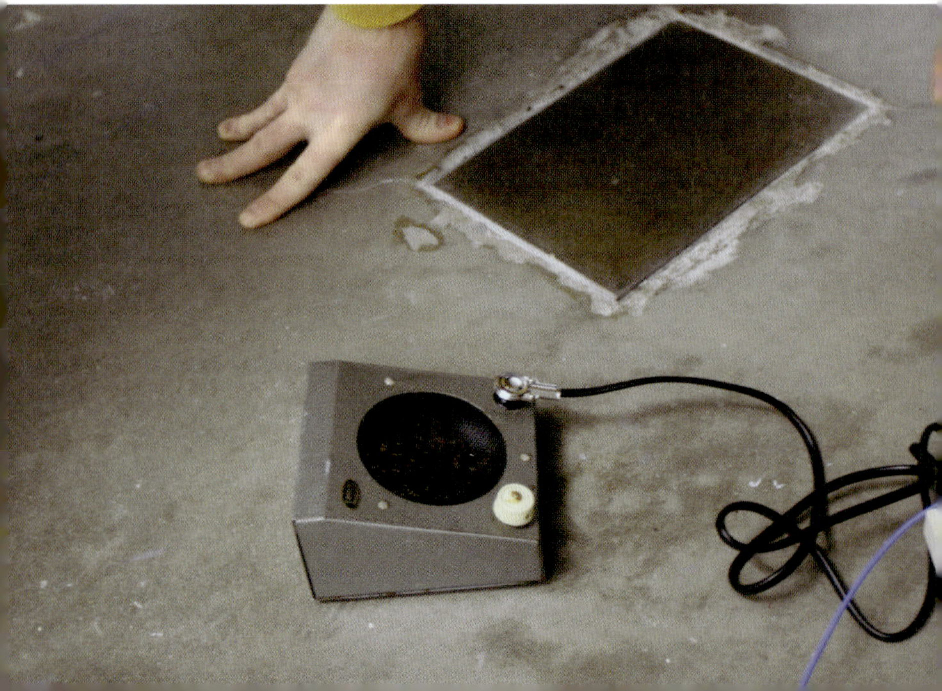

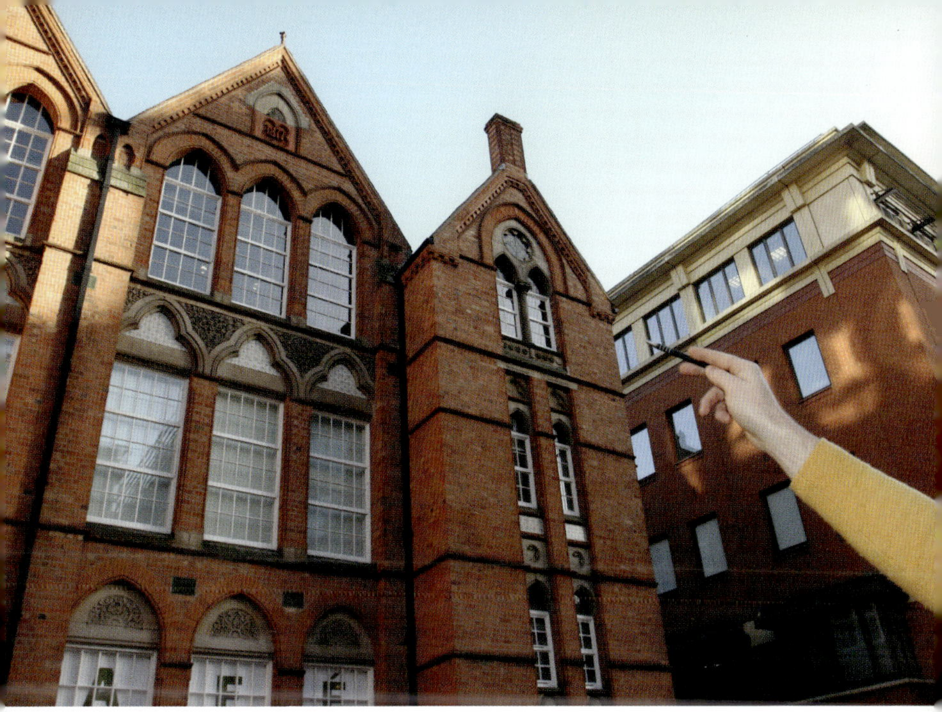

How to Use Fool's Gold (Pyrite Radio), production tests, Ikon Gallery, Birmingham, 2012
Pyrite, wood, safety pin, paperclip, bulldog clips, plastic drainpipe, electrical wire, bakelite headphones (passive crystal radio set with no built electrical components, earthed in the gallery with aerial extending outside)
Dimensions variable. With thanks to Geoffrey Roberts
Mystery Crystal Radio circuit diagram, first published by Proton in *The Sunday Mail*, Brisbane, 1932 (facing page)

How to Use Fool's Gold (Spectrum as a Mineral), 2011
Email correspondence with Tim Forde
UK frequency spectrum allocations, derived from OFCOM's Frequency Allocation Table (following pages)

From: Tim Forde
Date: Fri, Jul 1, 2011 at 1:48 PM
Subject: RE: Spectrum... A Mineral?
To: Sarah Browne

Hi Sarah,

Well, re. minerals. That was a bit of a slip of the tongue.

Article 10 of the Irish Constitution reads:

1. All natural resources, including the air and all forms of potential energy, within the jurisdiction of the Parliament and Government established by this Constitution and all royalties and franchises within that jurisdiction belong to the State subject to all estates and interests therein for the time being lawfully vested in any person or body.

2. All land and all mines, minerals and waters which belonged to Saorstát Éireann immediately before the coming into operation of this Constitution belong to the State to the same extent as they then belonged to Saorstát Éireann.

3. Provision may be made by law for the management of the property which belongs to the State by virtue of this Article and for the control of the alienation, whether temporary or permanent, of that property.

4. Provision may also be made by law for the management of land, mines, minerals and waters acquired by the State after the coming into operation of this Constitution and for the control of the alienation, whether temporary or permanent, of the land, mines, minerals and waters so acquired.

All governments make the same assertions in law. So, national governments, and then by extension the UN's International Telecommunications Union (ITU) assert the right and power to regulate its use at either a national or international level.

However, as a mineral, spectrum is different in some respects.

The amount of any mineral in existence is generally finite. Therefore, revenues accruing from licences to mine that mineral are generally once-off affairs. Spectrum is a resource that renews itself and so revenues can accrue from it indefinitely. Changing uses of the resource will affect the revenues earned and fees charged for access.

The amount of spectrum available is also finite, but in a different way. Radio spectrum is considered to be the frequencies between 3 kHz to 300 GHz . The usefulness of these frequencies varies depending on the application to which you want to put the spectrum. There is a so-called 'sweet spot' of spectrum for mobile use which is more valuable because its properties (currently) require hardware, i.e. the radios, the size of which are suited to carrying in your pocket. An analogy here maybe with different grades of coal, oil or gold etc. They are only good for certain purposes at different grades. Like cold, oil, etc., spectrum can be put to 'better' use, i.e. more economically efficient use, if the technology is developed to do so. For coal, oil this means newer, more efficient power stations, etc. that get more energy out of the fuel or can use lower grade fuel. For spectrum, this means developing radios that can use less bandwidth, less power etc to transmit the same/more information. Or developing radios that can use spectrum outside the favoured sweet spot.

However, a big difference between spectrum and any other mineral or natural resource such as land, water, air, metals, etc. is that spectrum is infinitely renewing in time and cannot be destroyed or tampered with. By that I mean that if you do something bad with a radio now, causing interference and destroying someone else's spectrum usage or your own, once you stop doing whatever was causing that interference the spectrum returns to its perfect, clean, state again. There are no lingering effects. [We'll ignore the claims of radios causing cancer for now.]

So unlike every other resource which dwindles to nothing or requires decontamination, or active recycling, spectrum instantly recycles itself for fresh new use. *

Rambling....... if you have more directed questions, let me know.

Tim

CTVR - The Telecommunications Research Centre
Trinity College, Dublin,
Ireland
www.ctvr.ie

Radio service legend

- Shared civil military use
- Civil use
- Military use

- Radio astronomy
- Aeronautical radionavigation
- Earth exploration – satellite
- Amateur
- Aeronautical mobile
- Maritime mobile
- Maritime radionavigation
- Radio navigation
- Meteorological aids
- Broadcasting
- Broadcasting – satellite
- Fixed
- Fixed satellite service
- Amateur – satellite
- Inter-satellite
- Mobile satellite
- Land mobile
- Radio location
- Space research
- Space operation
- Mobile
- Standard frequency and time signal
- Standard frequency and time signal satellite
- Meteorological satellite
- Radionavigation satellite

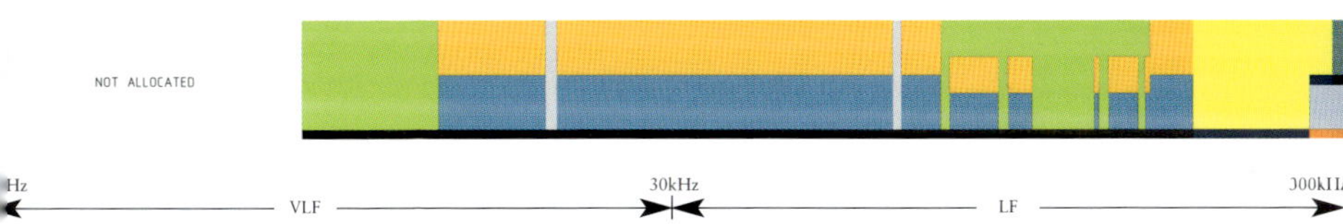
NOT ALLOCATED
Hz
VLF
30kHz
LF
300kHz

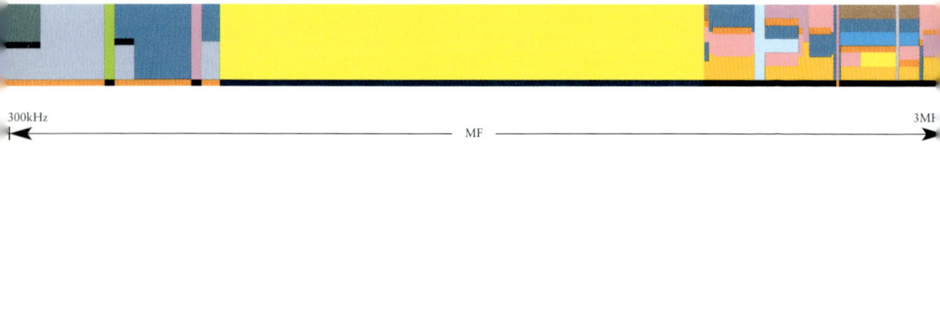
300kHz
MF

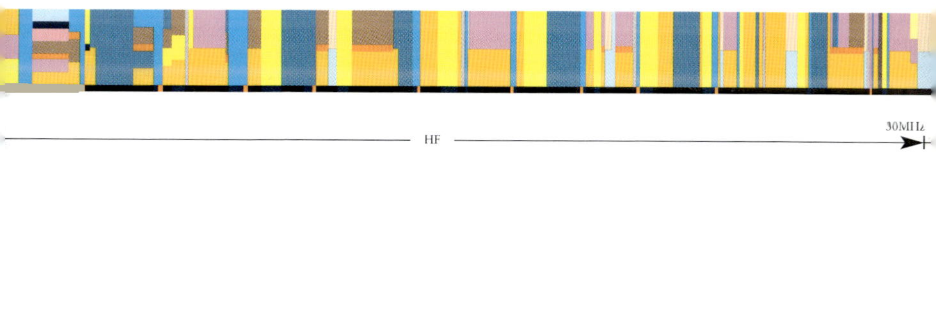
HF
30MHz

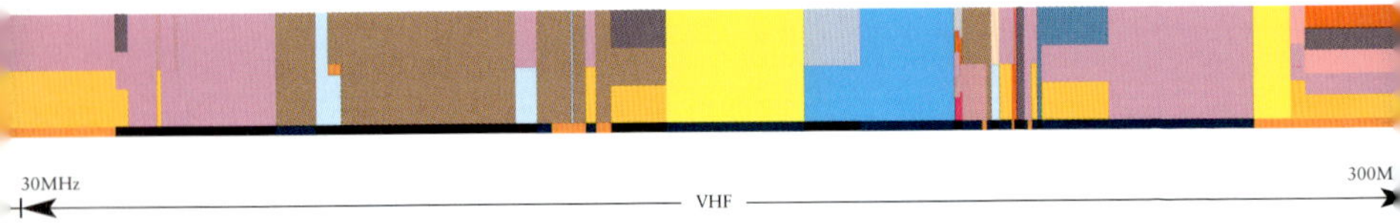
30MHz
VHF
300M

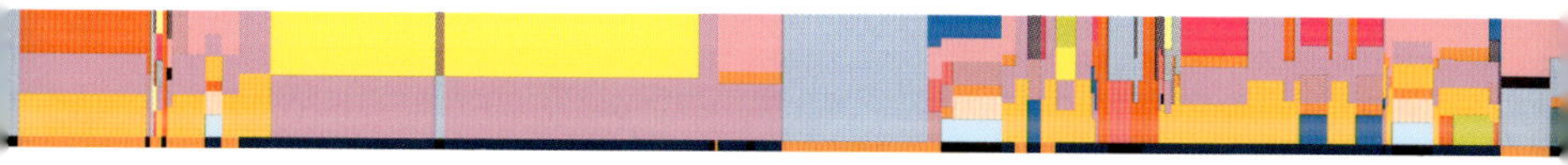

UHF
1GHz
L
2GHz
3GHz

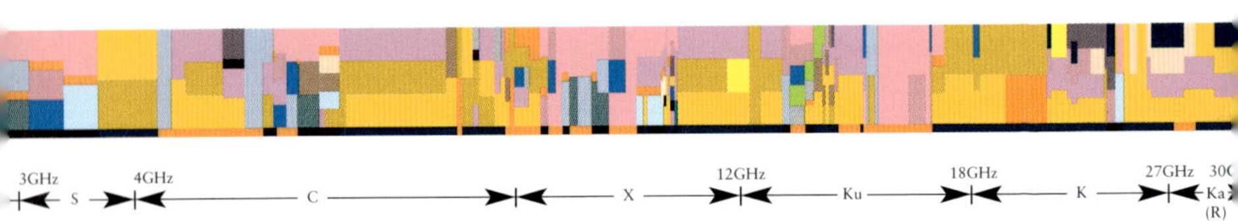
3GHz
S
4GHz
C
X
12GHz
Ku
18GHz
K
27GHz
30
Ka
(R)

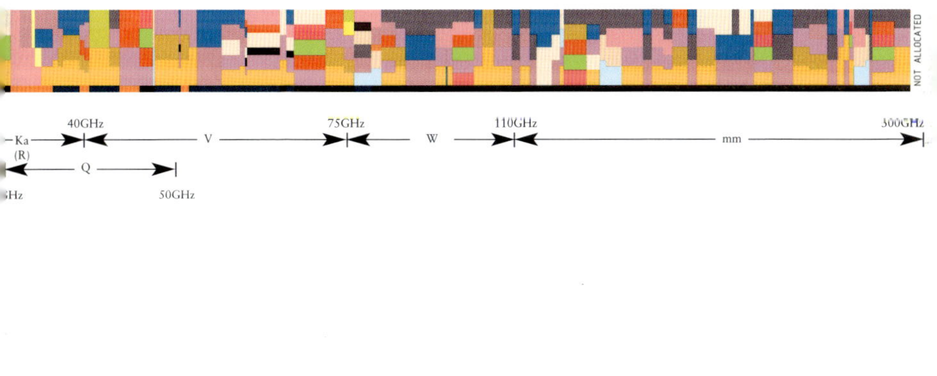
NOT ALLOCATED
40GHz
75GHz
110GHz
300GHz
Ka
(R)
V
W
mm
Q
50GHz

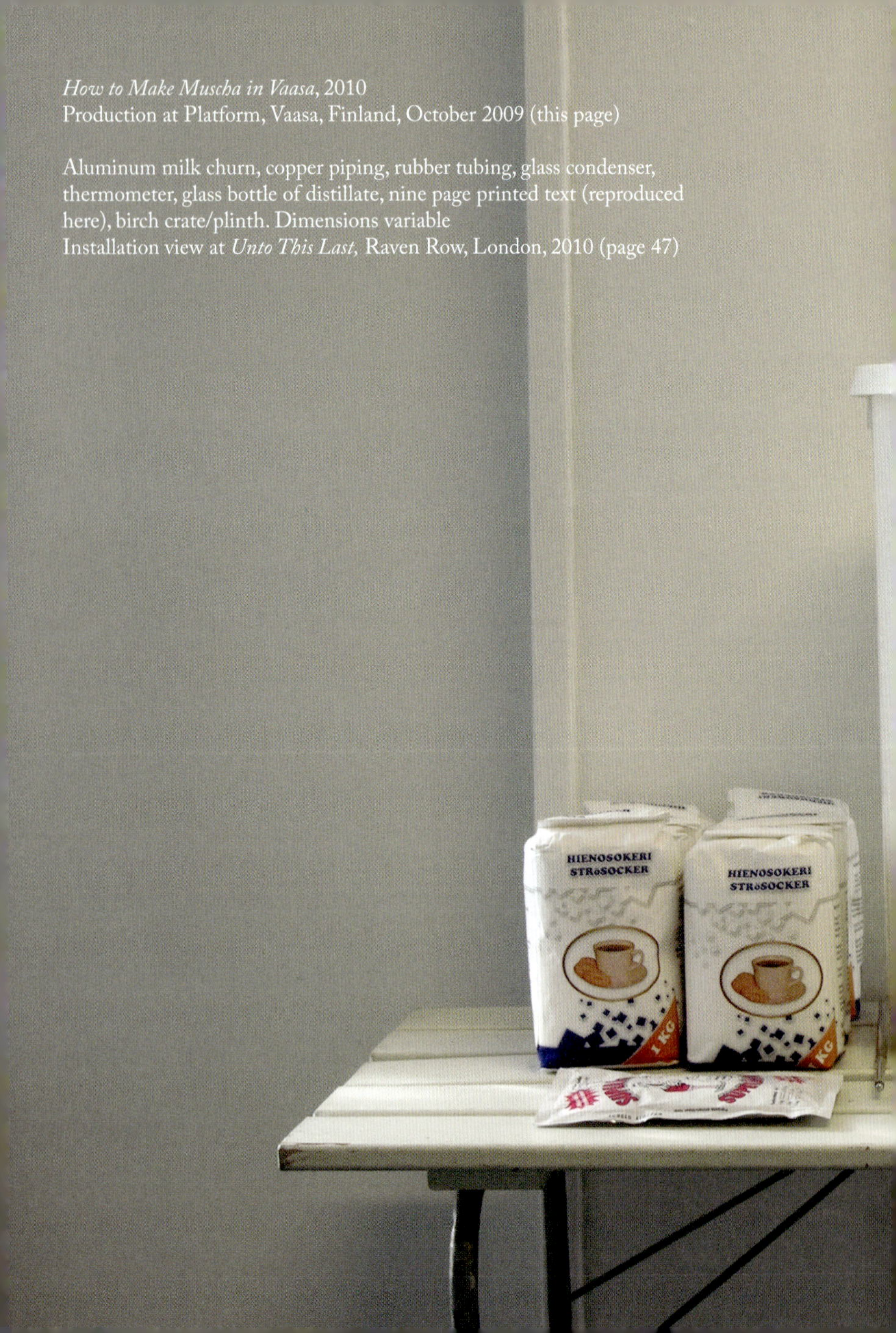

How to Make Muscha in Vaasa, 2010
Production at Platform, Vaasa, Finland, October 2009 (this page)

Aluminum milk churn, copper piping, rubber tubing, glass condenser, thermometer, glass bottle of distillate, nine page printed text (reproduced here), birch crate/plinth. Dimensions variable
Installation view at *Unto This Last,* Raven Row, London, 2010 (page 47)

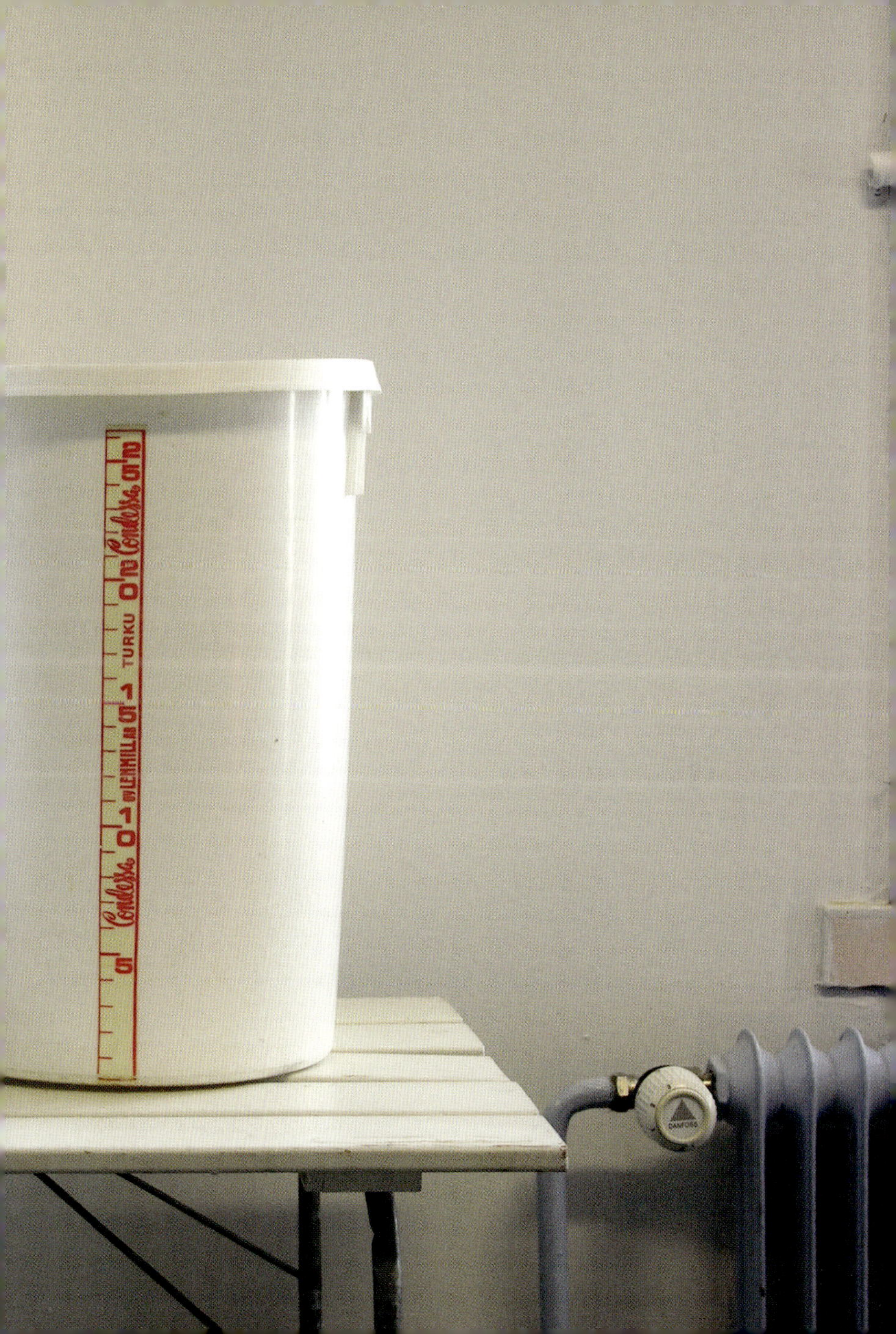
TURKU
DANFOSS

HOW TO MAKE MUSCHA IN VAASA

The simplest still to build is a stove-top pot still. A wash of sugar, water, nutrients & yeast will distill to a flavourless & odourless spirit (muscha).

Secure collaborators.[1]

Acquire a good recipe: seek out local knowledge.[2]

Either follow up or ignore all folklore on the subject.[3]

Procure the necessary materials.[4]

Find a place to brew the mash & distill.[5]

Consider a defence.[6]

1. In order of appearance:

Jukka
Maria N
Marcus
Dragos
Trissan
Hasse
Ulrika
Uffe
Tobias
Peppe
Jaakko
Ronan
Maria Å

This artwork has been co-produced with Platform, Vaasa, Finland.

2. Issues of language and translation are key to this endeavour. "Making muscha in Vaasa" is an activity that is highly locally-specific, but also a general proposal that can be transposed to other contexts.

It is Jukka who tells me that there is a Finnish dialect word for what I'm trying to make, *muscha*, from moonshine – Finnish immigrants to the US learned how to make it in the Prohibition era. Kilju [*KILLyou*] seems to be a similar slang word in Swedish but refers to the initial brew (mash) that is then distilled to make muscha. Since the region of Ostrobothnia hosts a large population of Finnish Swedes, there is some confusion about the respective terms and their origins.

Maria tells me that there is a recipe in the gallery 'somebody' left for me. She sends it to me translated into English: I need to get it translated back so that I will be able to buy the ingredients in the shop. It turns out to be only a recipe for the mash and I think I've already found a simpler way to do that.

Marcus helps me translate packaging labels so that I can buy the correct yeast. Dragos and Trissan help me to translate the instructions on the packet. The packaging for the turbo yeast is careful to instruct that the fruit quantity must be greater than the quantity of sugar added, and emphasizes that to start fermentation with only sugar and water is illegal.

'Local knowledge' may also be accessed extensively through the internet.

3. Jukka tells me that I am in the muscha-making capital of Finland, even though no one talks about it. He describes how he first noticed something was happening after moving here when he saw the vast amounts of turbo yeast at his local hardware store.

Hasse explains that taxes on alcohol are due to increase again soon and he predicts that people will once again start distilling at home – it hasn't been that popular in recent years. He tells me a story about a house a friend of his was renovating where the floorplan didn't match the building. After significant confusion and investigation, it turned out there was a false wall and a secret room for a muscha boiler.

Marcus tells me that he has a relative who makes muscha, but wouldn't be keen to talk about it. He says that he and Tobias, our neighbour, used to make beer together and he is curious about how the cooking works. Tobias outlines the memory of a scandal a few years ago when there was an evening course in distilling (only water). There was a big clamour about it but he can't remember what the eventual legal outcome was and if the course was cancelled or not.

Ulrika and her cousin Uffe have a story about another "evening course" run on an island somewhere where the police came and did successfully confiscate the still that the group made. That was years ago though, and they can't remember the details. She says she kind of knows an ironsmith who might be cooking some and growing some things, but she isn't sure of his name and he lives kind of far away.

Jukka tells me a story about a house that was plumbed in such a way that the entire building worked as a giant still. The pipes were contained within the walls and the muscha production doubled as a central heating system.

4. I ask Hasse if there is a wine- or beer-making shop around. He tells me that there isn't, but Ronan tells me I should be able to get things in one of the supermarkets. We go to one that is run by some kind of Christian corporation, so they don't have anything to do with booze – a remnant of Prohibition [*kieltolaki*] and the temperance movement [*raittiusliike*].

Tobias is really helpful. He lends me a big plastic tub to ferment the mash and some other equipment that he has lying around his workshop in the soap factory – thermometers and condensers and things. Marcus recommends the bigger supermarket across the bridge. It's great, they have lots of things I was worried about getting like rubber grommets and an airlock and hygrometer.

I get most of the ingredients I need from the supermarket but still need to get or make a boiler, the most important part, and some copper piping. Peppe tells me he knows a plumber, Jaakko, who used to make muscha and would give me some for cheap if I told him he had sent me. Jaakko lives somewhere else, so he arranges for me to meet his wife, who is visiting her brother, who lives a bit closer in a house in the countryside. It's quite strange to meet her there as she arrives with her huge car full of children and a smallish coil of copper piping, even stranger when I hand over a handful of coins. The copper has been used for something before, but I don't know what.

I try a catering shop to find something for the boiler, but it's pricey for what they are offering, and none of the *kirpputori* [indoor fleamarkets] have anything that would be big enough, not even the army surplus store. Ronan, who used to work for the props department in the theatre, takes me to a really big one on the edge of the town; it's full of intriguing objects and obsolete technologies, but no suitable big pot. Cycling into the studio the next morning I spot a perfect smaller version outside a little antik shop and snap it up. It should be easier to manage, and safer in the kitchen. I work really hard all day and am frustrated when I get to Alko [the state-controlled alcohol shop] ten minutes after it closes at 8pm. No wine with dinner tonight.

Ronan brings me to a shop that deals exclusively in rubber items – *gummi*. They stock an incredible variety of tubing, wheels, valves, grommets and sheeting, all in a selection of colours, grades and gauges. The smell in the shop is intoxicating. Ronan helps by speaking to the men in Finnish and I leave with a couple of grommets for the lid of the still, precisely the correct diameter, measured closely with a calipers. There are a number of further visits needed, without Ronan to translate. I variously bring with me an aluminium lid with a hole in it, a roll of copper piping, and a wrapped up glass condenser. Finally I need to bring rudimentary drawings detailing the diameter of taps and explaining the different water sources, directions, and gauge of pipe needed. The older gentleman, who previously didn't seem to speak English at all, twinkles and breaks out with 'We know what you are doing you know!' After that himself and his colleague crack into action, one explaining the list and the other fetching things and checking measurements of each item. There is an atmosphere of supportive collusion. I leave with everything I need.

5. Dragos wants to know where I'll be cooking and is worried about the smell in the studios (we are neighbours) even though he doesn't say so in so many words. This isn't something I had considered. He also wants to know if they can keep the cooking kit when I finish – I tell him no, I'll have to have it to exhibit as a piece of work.

After the sugar is dissolved in the hot water, it seems to take forever for the mixture in the tub to cool below 25C – I'm using one of those stick-on acquarium thermometers that probably isn't very accurate. If the mixture is too hot it will stress or kill the yeast, but if it's too cold the yeast won't be activated at all. Hours later, it's cool enough to pitch the yeast. It's early in the morning by the time I'm ready to leave the studio: the streets are dark and deserted outside the window, and with Johnny Cash playing inside, it feels suitably illicit.

The next day the studio is filled with a sweet, sticky aroma, and the air is gurgling softly. The yeast is alive in the big swollen plastic tub; it's breathing up through the airlock. After about a day and a half of fermenting, the yeast is used up and the mash is ready for distillation. Ronan helps me bring it back home, where there is a cooker and better ventilation for any unpleasant odours and poisonous fumes.

The still is set up on a cooker hob and a thermometer is inserted through a hole in the top, to measure the temperature of the steam. The copper pipe is inserted through another hole on the lid and threaded through the condenser. The distillate should drip through into a glass bowl in the sink. Plastic tubing connects the cold water tap to the input of the condenser, and flows out through it into the sink. It looks like a kind of plug-in to the kitchen.

The principle is simple: Boil the mash (which is around 14% alcohol) and condense the vapour to retrieve a liquid with a higher concentration of alcohol. This pure spirit is then diluted to a drinkable percentage.

However there is a lot of room for variation with custom-made stills and there are some dangers. For example, the angle of the lyne arm (the copper pipe extending from the top of the still) will determine how much internal reflux occurs: the less internal reflux, the fewer compounds stripped out and the fuller the flavour. Variation of temperature makes a difference. Patience is important and greediness – trying to collect the maximum distillate – is dangerous because the 'heads' and 'tails' (the first and last compounds that are distilled, more and less volatile than ethanol respectively) are poisonous. When consumed they cause a range of ill effects, ranging on a spectrum from a bad hangover to blindness to death.

Therefore, it is recommended to drink the results of your labour yourself before sharing it.

6. There are a number of possible defences for illegal domestic tinkering.

a) Thrift

b) Libertarianism/ Anarchism

(In this and all cases of defying sumptuary laws, the defence may be strengthened if the spirit produced is not for resale.)

c) Heritage

'If water, vodka, and sauna does not help, the condition is fatal.' (Finnish proverb)

Among the first pioneer settlers to the USA were the semi-nomadic Finnish *kirvesmiehet* [axe-wielders]. They would loose hogs to feed in the coniferous forests and tear through the timber, building shelters with the remaining logs. Scorching the earth with fire, they scattered rye seeds among the stumps and settled there until harvest; then the rye would be distilled into spirits and the settlers would move on to another area. Each immigrant community had its own distilling traditions that often related to social and bodily rituals, such as saunas and sweat lodges.

In Vaasa's Ostrobothnian Museum, there is a small section that shows lots of old glass bottles and discusses moonshining and Prohibition in Finland briefly. Apparently during the time of the great fire in Vaasa in 1852, moonshine ran down the streets. Distilling is presented as a kind of vernacular knowledge, or a quaint form of resistance, but one that is quite safely in the past. However, contemporary distilling is active in the overlap between cottage industry and artisanal craft.

d) Art

The use of art as an alibi may be weakened in that it implicitly rests on an idea of the artist as a foreigner, and ignorance of the law is no excuse. However:

'All ideas are art if they are concerned with art and fall within the conventions of art' (SL); and further, art may enact peculiar transformations of state in the status and qualities of substances.

Appendix: Notes for installation

A. Crate/ Plinth

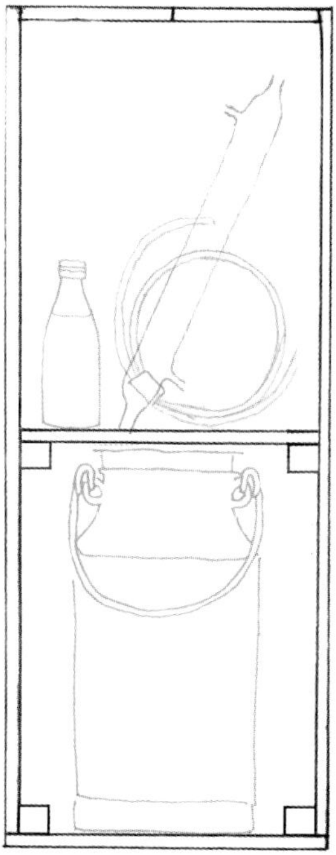

- Base of plinth is removable in two halves; one is used as display shelf
- Condenser, thermometer, tublin, fittings, bottle of muscha
  Packing stored inside plinth during exhibition
- Removable interior shelf
  Accessed through base
- Still (aluminium milk churn)
- Top of crate is pinned and sealed shut. For shipping the crate is transported with the base facing upwards and is unpacled from this angle

B. Still

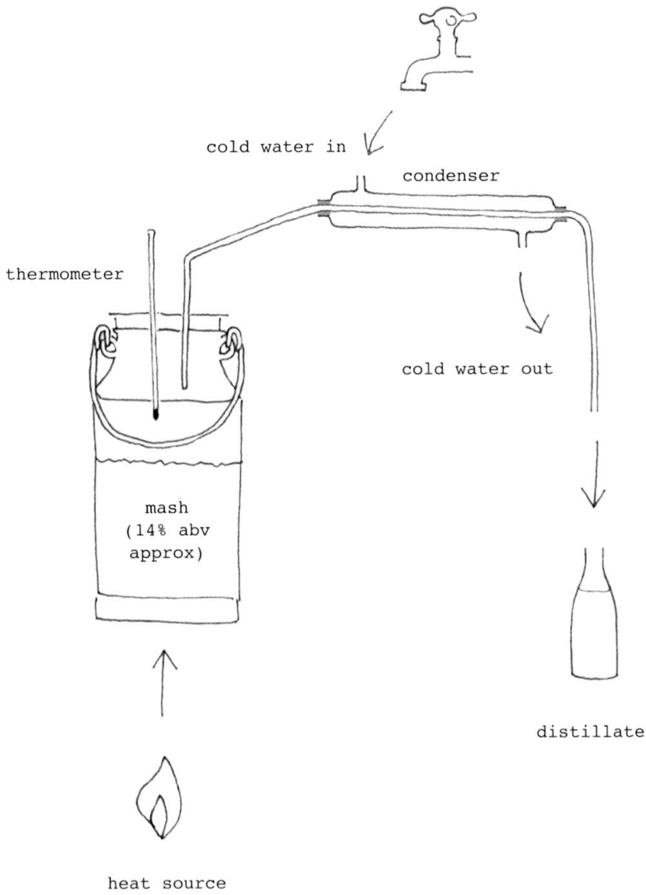
cold water in
condenser
thermometer
cold water out
mash
(14% abv
approx)
distillate
heat source

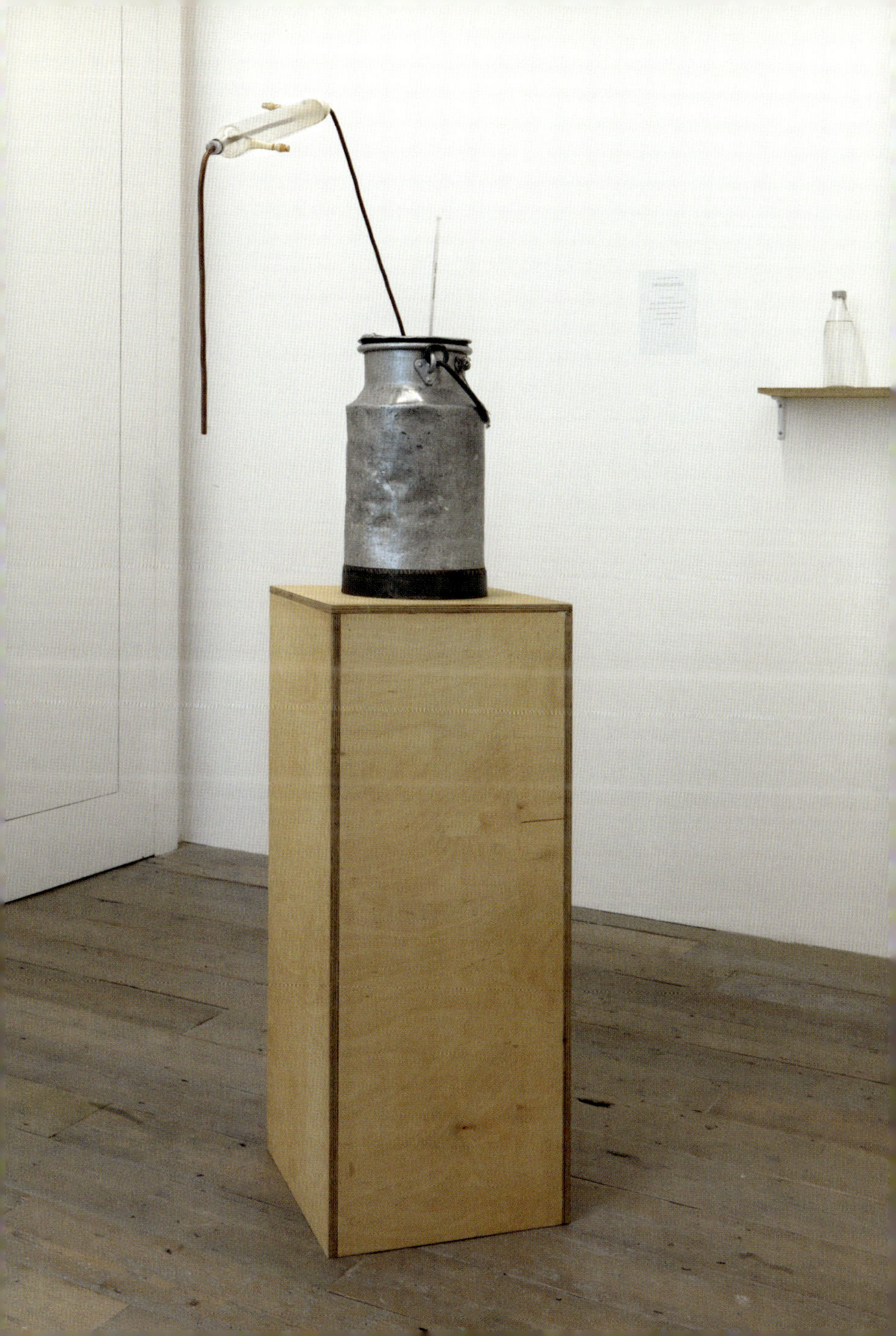

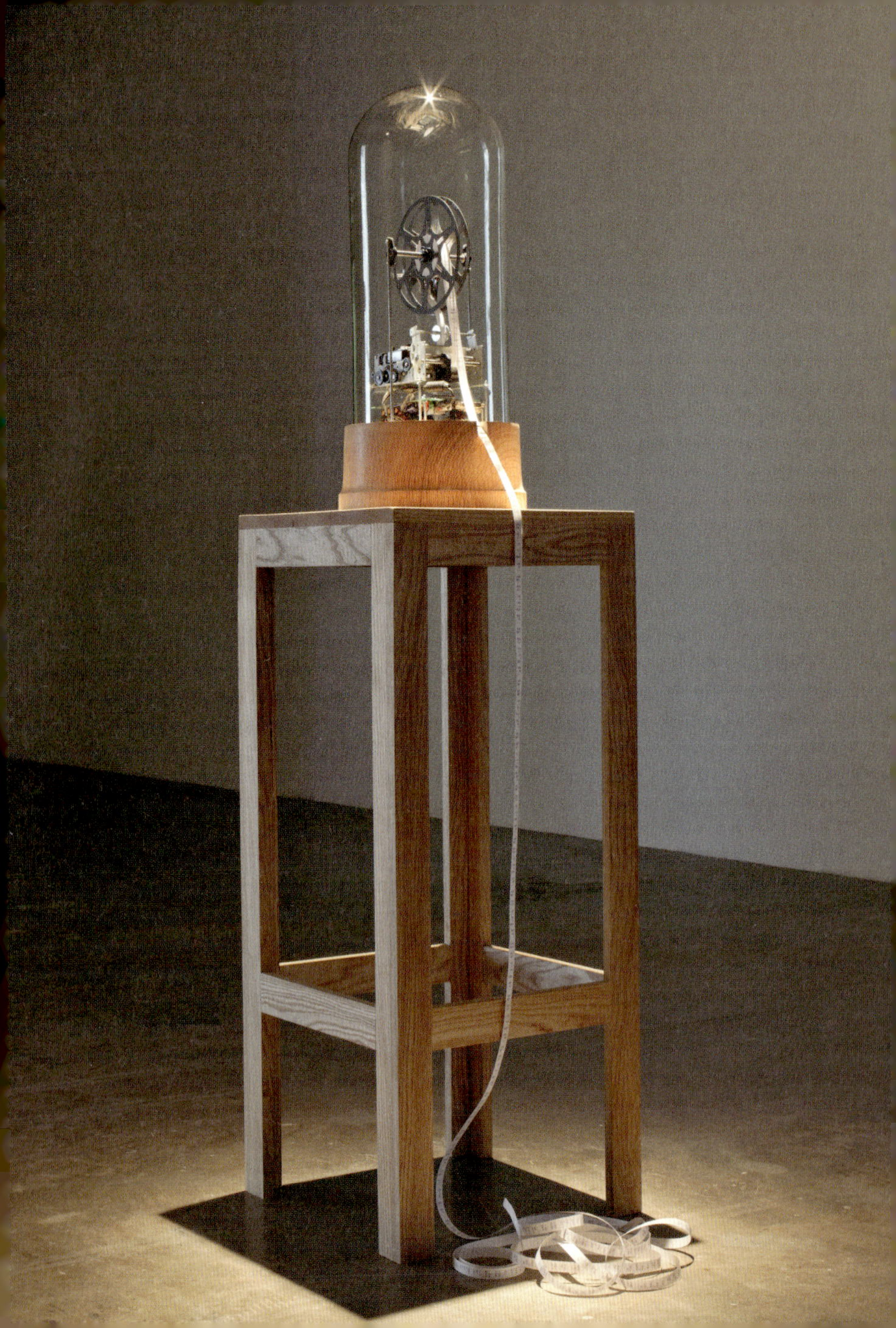

On Aesthetics, Economies and Commemorations (or the work of Sarah Browne)

Tessa Giblin

Artistic research as experimental aesthetics is ultimately characterised by the continuous movement between fluidity and rigidity, laboratory and herbarium, smooth space and striated space, non-discipline and discipline, the particular and the universal.

—Henk Slager [1]

Experimental Aesthetics

Abstract or conceptual reasoning, and fluid movement from the fantastical to the irrational or from the concrete to the tantalisingly obtuse, are both treasured qualities of contemporary art. Contemporary art is full of open concepts that provide escape routes which can in turn lead to some kind of original thought, but they often require a gesture of faith. The type of knowledge embedded in or accessed through contemporary art is not often empirical, nor is it always trusted. It is more like a belief system or a faith. If we chose to opt in, to surrender our scepticism (or indeed embrace it), a world of contemplation and relativism can open up, a world which the rest of our daily encounters can at times actively attempt to inhibit. This conceptual liberation has been one of the driving attractions of a field of art-making and thinking, characterised more often by non-knowledge than knowledge, by riddles than equations. Yet over these last two years, we have come face to face with another system of abstraction and obfuscation, a system also characterised by open concepts and conceptual reasoning, and bought into by an act of faith or belief on the part of a great number of its constituents. This is the world of finance, the economy, the great, abstract web of real and non-real transactions, monies and equations which form the bedrock of the crisis currently lived.

The relationships in Sarah Browne's *Second Burial at Le Blanc* oscillate between an experimental artistic thinking and an effort to map what the single shared currency means to us in Europe. The piece confronts the ways in which we can conceive of its implications against a backdrop of micro-economies, the development of international financial transactions through the lens of Wall Street and the idea of exchange as an over-arching, multi-faceted concept. It is a sculpture, a 16mm film and a newspaper publication, and is developing and evolving as it roves between Dublin, Birmingham, Le Blanc, Vancouver and perhaps beyond. *Second Burial at Le Blanc* is a memorial, a ritual, a commemoration and a funeral, and it is an artwork, a film, an essay and a gift.

Ireland is an example of a country for which the long struggle towards sovereignty still provides the foundation of cultural and national identities. This hard-won independence is today fiercely protected by citizens and is part of the reason why Ireland alone voted no (by referendum) to ratifying the Lisbon Treaty in 2008. A year later this decision was rectified by a pro-Europe referendum campaign mounted by Ireland's government, which stressed Ireland's freedom, sovereignty and autonomy, and put the negative result of the previous referendum down to a lack of information and knowledge on behalf of the voters. *Second Burial at Le Blanc* exhibited at Project Arts Centre, Dublin in May 2011, a stone's throw from the Central Bank of Ireland, was inevitably identified with the crisis of the Irish economy in 2009/10 and in part read within this broader cultural referent. This European emergency has since expanded to encompass Portugal, Spain and Greece in 2011, with the possibility of future loan defaults underscoring the insecurity of EU member states' relationships to their common currency, the euro. The International Monetary Fund also appears as a spectre in the background to this story, with France the first nation to accept a loan from the IMF in 1947, and Ireland the most recent in 2011.

Micro-economies

Browne's research and resulting artworks are foils through which we can approach the conceptual complexity of the known unknowns that litter our economic landscape, and as such become just as elusive as the scenario they symbolise.

Le Blanc, the central character in Browne's project, is a small town in central France. In an effort to reboot its local economy, its local artisans and traders in recent years created a scheme to provide goods in exchange for the long-replaced currency, the franc. Since France adopted the euro as a single shared currency in 2002, the Banque de France has set the 17th February 2012 as a deadline, until which time franc banknotes will continue to be accepted by them in exchange for euro. Le Blanc merchants and shop keepers have capitalised on this window of opportunity. As well as providing a niche service to 'hoarders and accumulators' of the nostalgic currency, they have promoted their boutique exchange industry as a point of difference, hoping to attract tourists and visitors who will inject wealth into the local economy. On visiting the Le Blanc traders' website artcomin.fr, a digital countdown clock is the first image encountered, which counts down the days, hours, minutes and seconds until the February deadline, the final moment that the Banque de France will accept exchange and the primary marketing tool for Artisanat Commerce Industrie Le Blanc (Art'Com'In) and businesses of the small town.

Despite being the central character, Le Blanc is not the only point in Browne's contextual collection to refer to micro-economies. In her newspaper publication printed in both English and French, *On Hoarding, Accumulating, and Gifting,* 2011 (freely distributed in Le Blanc and Dublin, and a version reproduced here) we are informed about other situations: "as of 3rd March 2011, a fishing village called Mugardos in northern Spain has decided to reintroduce the old currency—the peseta—alongside the euro in a bid to encourage purchases in times of severe recession."[2] There is also the currency of the island of Yap in the Caroline Islands of the Pacific Ocean, obsolete for the past 40 years. Called *Rai,* the beautiful symbolic currency attributed value to each of the huge limestone rocks based on the difficulty of getting and transporting them to the island, sometimes a mortal danger in itself. These two examples summarise the devices or strategies with which Browne brings her research constellation into the space of artistic contemplation: not an essay, cohesive argument or even particularly joined-up thinking, *On Hoarding, Accumulating, and Gifting* is more a staccato collection of anecdotes – some more and some less informing the film and sculpture at the centre of the artwork, favouring a plurality of intelligences over a direct thrust towards academic journalism. Moreover, the newspaper is a visual essay, communicating as much in its editing of images (both found and by Browne) as in the brief captions that accompany them.

The Commemoration

Browne attributes some inspiration for the project to the anthropologist Marshall Sahlins, referencing his publication *Stone Age Economics* in *On Hoarding, Accumulating, and Gifting*. Ideas are extracted that she finds relevant, partly as a provocation within the overall logic of *Second Burial at Le Blanc*, rather than as wholesale prescription to such theories. He states, "To understand our [western] economy requires the same kind of anthropological sensibility we bring to the study of others."[3] For Browne, this call for an ethnographic approach to the interrogation of developed countries' economic entanglement is illustrated by the story of the *Rai* and echoed in the ritualised performance made in Le Blanc, the subject of her 16mm film. Browne's procession through the streets of Le Blanc is a symbolic transition which leads a small group of local people from the old part of the city to the new. They carry on their shoulders a primitive stretcher and the event is filmed on increasingly anachronistic 16mm film stock. Perched on top of the stretcher is the ticker-tape countdown clock, the functioning sculpture that was the centrepiece of the exhibition at Project Arts Centre, which will be shown to a gallery public for the final time at the opening of her exhibition at Ikon Gallery, Birmingham, before departing for Le Blanc and its final exorcism. Housed in a domed glass case, the device is one of the many hybrid objects or concepts in the work and amalgamates analogue and digital technologies. A discarded receipt-printer is adapted into a live-feed receiver of fluctuating currency data via wireless internet, printing the comparative exchange rates of the euro to franc (fixed) and euro to US dollar (variable). The printout also relays a live countdown to the 17th February 2012 in days, hours, minutes and seconds.

While on display in the gallery, the ticker-tape continuously amassed during the day, creating cascades of thin white paper which fell down the sides of the wooden plinth and pooled on the floor. Carried atop the stretcher through the streets of Le Blanc, the sculpture became more of an image of that transaction—a weird hybrid thing entangled with the history and extrapolation of its own use value—both as primary resource and as secondary, discarded material.

The original ticker-tape machines produced endless snakes of paper strips, as stock market data from all over the world was transmitted via telegraph to trading floors and information boards. This by-product of the financial markets found a secondary use as celebrational confetti, appearing for the first time in 1886 when streams of ticker-tape were spontaneously flung from high-rise windows during the parade that welcomed the Statue of Liberty, a gift from France to the city of New York. With the idea of a 'ticker-tape parade' now commonly recognised throughout the world, Browne conflates the concept of financial trade with another mixed message of technological development, creating a procession for the machine which once provided the by-product used to celebrate these processions.

As Susan George and Fabrizio Sabelli write about the World Bank in the introduction to *Faith and Credit: the World Bank's Secular Empire*:

> The multiple roles it plays and the many functions of power it assumes, like the difficulty of defining it, make the Bank a total social phenomenon, a Thing. This is why [...] we have spoken of beliefs, faith, doctrine, prophecy, and fundamentalism; of ancestors' initiation, esprit de corps, intellectual leadership and rule.

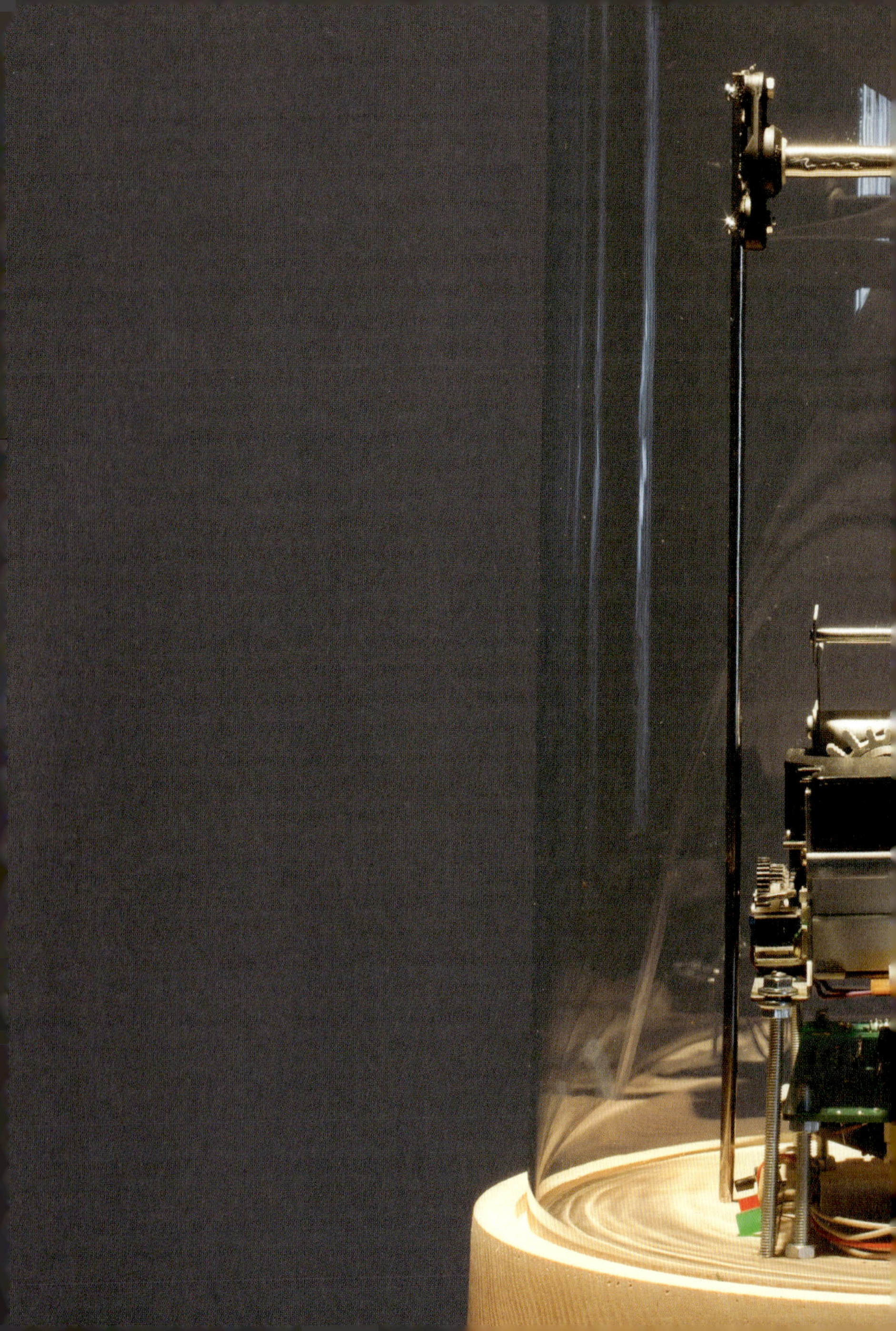

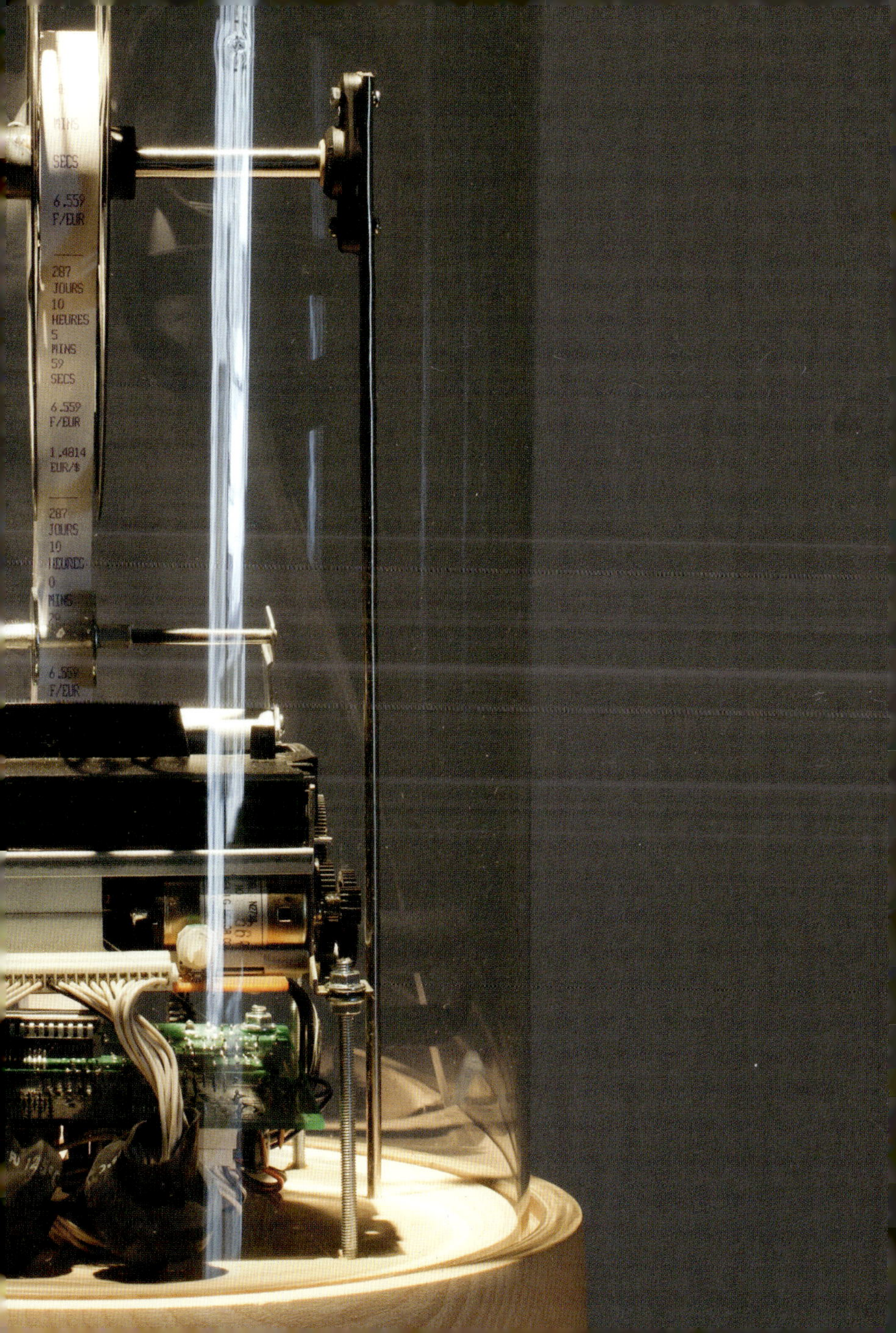
MINS
SECS
6.559
F/EUR
287
JOURS
10
HEURES
5
MINS
59
SECS
6.559
F/EUR
1.4814
EUR/$
287
JOURS
10
HEURES
0
MINS
6.559
F/EUR

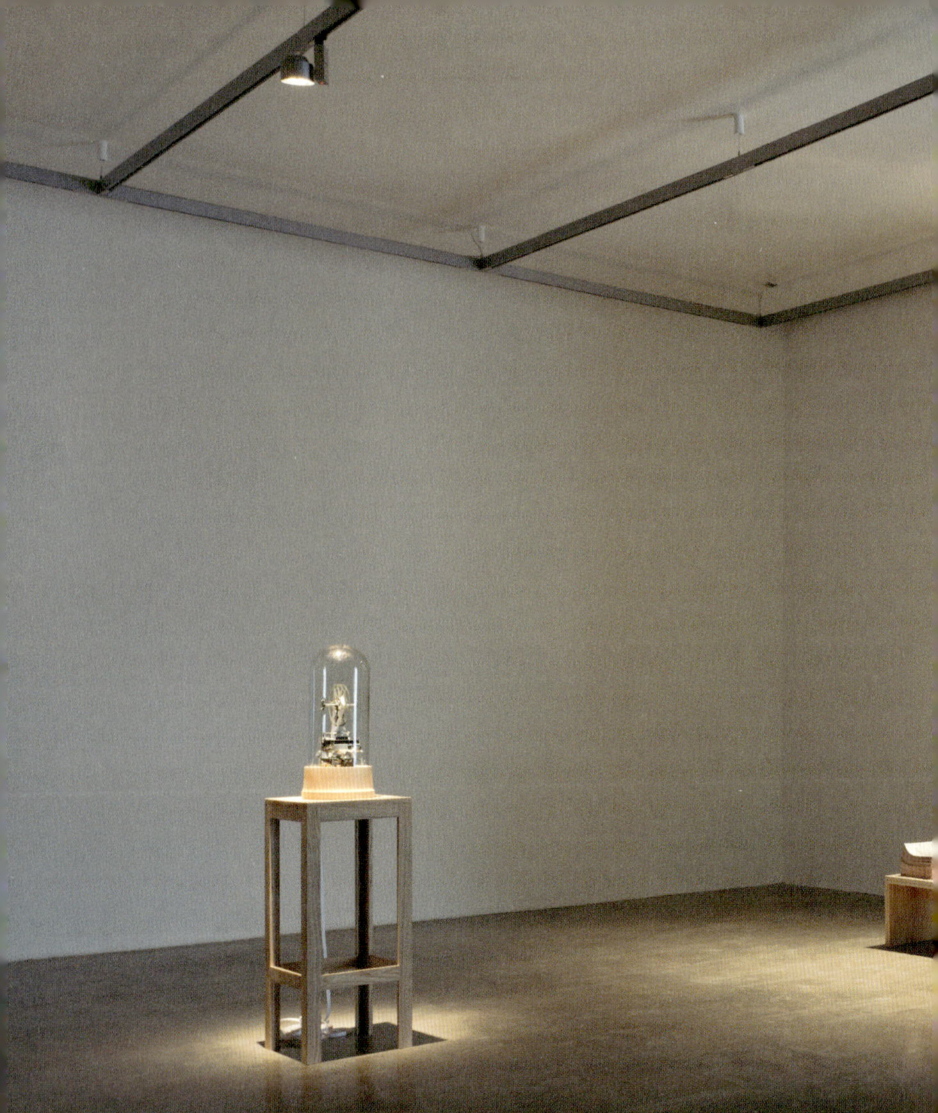

Second Burial at Le Blanc, 2011
16mm film, colour, silent, 8'18". Customised ticker-tape countdown clock, height 660mm, Ø300mm, length of paper variable (counting down the hours, minutes and seconds to the last francs to be exchanged on 17 February 2012, and live currency feed via wireless internet). Installation views at Project Arts Centre, Dublin

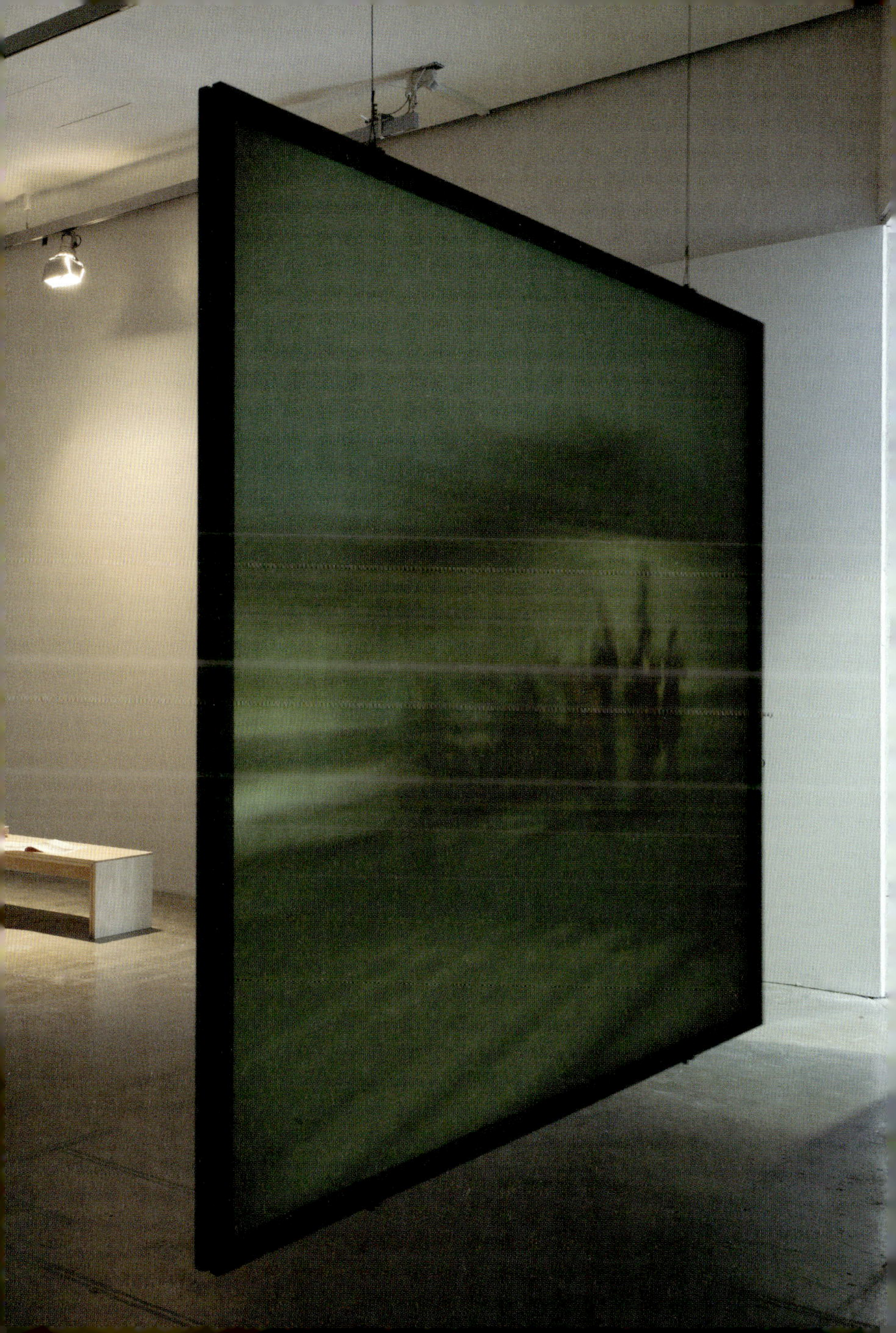

In explaining this "total social phenomenon", they argue that many people think we need it for the same reason we think we need the Church to govern a relationship with faith: "Frail, imperfect humanity needs constraints, guardrails, continual instruction in, and interpretation of, the doctrine."[4] This instructional and interpretive aspect of the ritual is expanded and in a sense freed by the associations drawn out in *On Hoarding, Accumulating, and Gifting.* Here we are introduced to the stories of other rituals: misinterpretations of the 'slow, majestic marching pace' of the French Legionnaires, or the detailed gifting of the Statue of Liberty to the US and the inaugural ticker-tape parade which resulted.

Nestled inside these pages is a further illuminating passage about the Madagascan ritualistic tradition of re-burial. The action of exhuming the dead, parading them around the town, informing them of interesting changes which may have occurred since their death, cleaning their bones and carefully re-shrouding them before re-interring them in an elaborate ceremony, underlines the beauty or respect involved in *Second Burial at Le Blanc*—the second burial of an almost-dead currency. More than just the documentation of a curious scenario, Browne created the film as a commemorative action. The artist built a memorial sculpture that marks a finite period of decline counting down to the 17th February 2012, but also produced a film which will outlast the context of its time. It provides a window into the past, a particular past in which we are living, creating a monument-in-process to the entangled ideological and historical moment that Le Blanc has come to represent.

Other Knotted Histories

The dedication to creating something new out of the knotted histories that fascinate her can also be seen in many of Browne's other works, particularly her project *Carpet for the Irish Pavilion at the Venice Biennale* (2009), which consisted of a custom made carpet, a 16mm black and white film, two drawings and a framed letter. This time her context is marked by the primary figure of Modernist designer and architect Eileen Gray. While excavating Gray's practice, personal biography and cultural position in modernist and Irish history, the work also plunges into territories of the niche industry, the now redundant economy of carpet making in Ireland, and the national cultural associations rife at both the Venice Biennale and in Gray's struggle with her Irish heritage. The materials and processes used to bring the artwork to life — from resurrected hand-knotting techniques in carpet making, to the use of 16mm film stock in filming the production of the carpet, to the type-written letter punched by the artist to the long dead Eileen Gray—are an earlier example of the type of mixed messages of technological development that return in *Second Burial at Le Blanc.* Continuously, Browne employs her own logic and devices in the making of the artwork, shifting the overall project from one of documentation to a new conceptual act of creation. This approach was alluded to with subtlety in her letter to Gray, framed and exhibited as part of the exhibition in Venice, in which she asks the deceased designer what she would think of the newly commissioned carpet:

> It looks somewhat like the series of yours also made by Donegal Carpets: the textured, un-cropped finish is the same; it is also being made with 9 knots to the square inch; and it will have a similarly limited colour palette arranged in single 'blocks'. Of course I do not have your theoretical or practical design experience. My design is based on volumes and areas of leftover colour from surplus wool stocks at the factory, so really the resemblance is only very superficial; the defining logics are quite different.[5]

Novel Models for Imagining Otherness

> Science is certainty; research is uncertainty. Science is supposed to be cold, straight, and detached; research is warm, involving, and risky. Science puts an end to the vagaries of human disputes; research creates controversies. Science produces objectivity by escaping as much as possible from the shackles of ideology, passions, and emotions; research feeds on all of those to render objects of inquiry familiar.[6]

One has to wonder, if we were to really engage with the Madagascan tradition of re-burial, to update the spirit of the deceased in relation to the changes in their village since their passage, what would we have to say to the spirit of the franc? Browne gives no answers, but she does create parameters within which one's own imagination can flourish. From German Chancellor Angela Merkel's authoritative statement, "The current crisis facing the euro is the biggest test Europe has faced in decades. It is an existential test and it must be overcome [...] if the euro fails, then Europe fails," to Marshall Sahlins' call for a realignment of the context of researching western economies to the anthropological approach taken in the study of 'other' cultures, Browne's parameters, or what I like to think of as a contextual constellation, is invested in uncertainty, risk, controversy and above all, imagination. As Slager states: "Artistic research practice seems to be an awareness of the urgency to draw attention to novel models for imagining otherness or to generate other forms of imagination through the potentiality of the artistic image in a time more than ever characterized by globalizing models of interpretation leaving hardly any room for difference and multiplicity."

Sarah Browne's commemoration envelopes time, arresting the massive wheels of progress and turning them back on themselves, asking not what the spirit of the franc would think of us now, but how we could account for and communicate the current situation to the spirit of the franc.

1 Henk Slager, *The Pleasure of Research,* (Helsinki: Finnish Academy of Fine Arts, 2001)

2 Sarah Browne, *On Hoarding, Accumulating and Gifting,* (Dublin: Project Press, First Edition 2011)

3 Marshall Sahlins, *Stone Age Economics,* (London: Routledge, 1972), p.xiii

4 Susan George and Fabrizio Sabelli, *Faith and Credit: The Worlds Bank's Secular Empire,* (Colorado: Westview Press, 1994), p.248

5 Sarah Browne, *Letter to Eileen Gray,* 2009, reproduced in *Sarah Browne,* (Carrick-on-Shannon; The Dock, 2009)

6 Bruno Latour, *From the World of Science to that of Research,* Science, Vol 280 No 5361 (April 1998), 208-209.

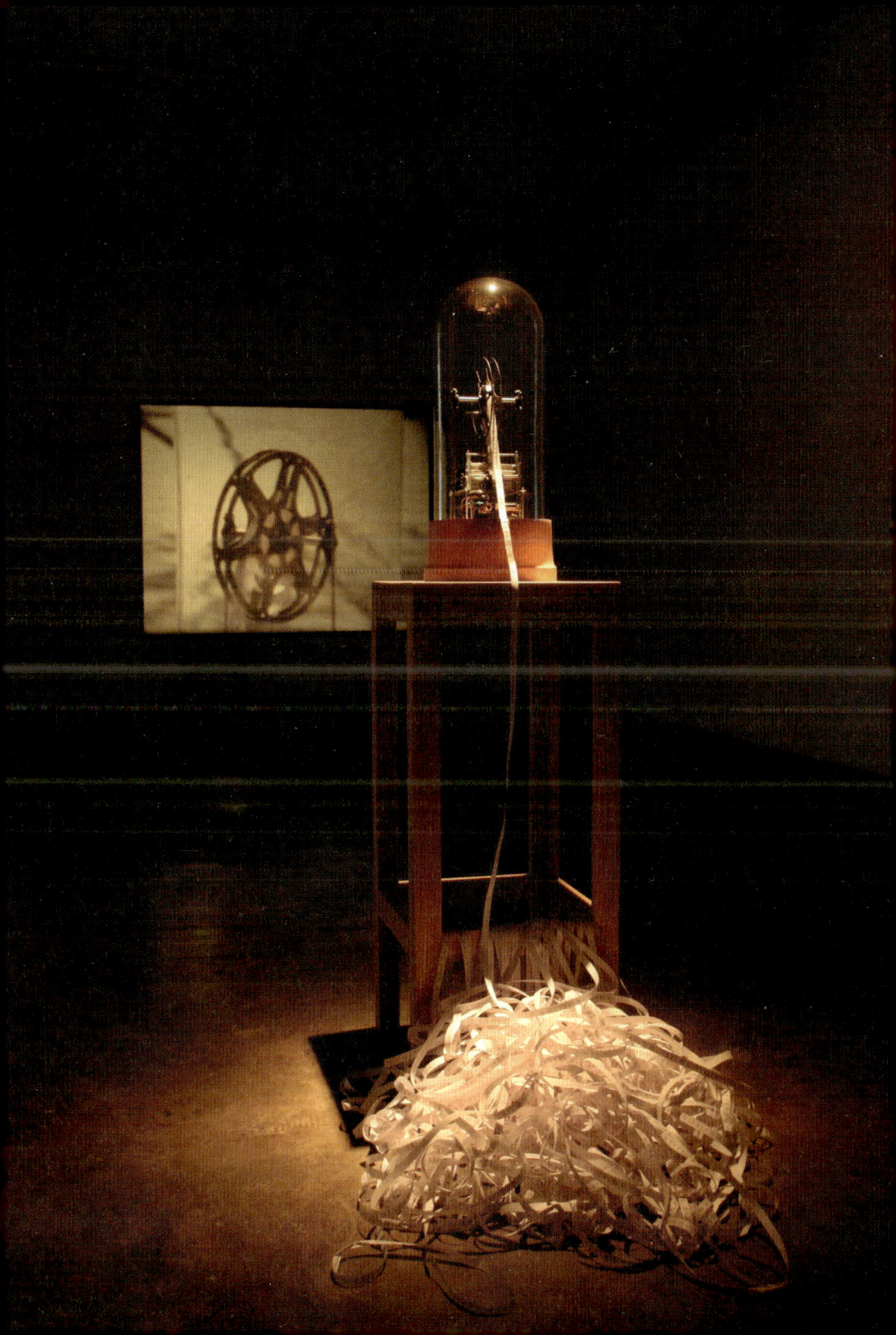

Carpet for the Irish Pavilion at the Venice Biennale, 2009
Surplus wool and linen stock from Donegal Carpets Factory
3000mm x 3000mm x 25mm
16mm film on DVD, b/w, silent, 18'03"

One Hour's Drawing for One Hour's Knotting (Sixteen Knots per Square Inch), 2009
One Hour's Drawing for One Hour's Knotting (Nine Knots per Square Inch), 2009
Two drawings with pencil and acrylic on paper, each 400mm x 300mm

Letter to Eileen Gray, 2009
Digital print on two pages of archival paper, 300mm x 400mm
(not shown)

All works commissioned for the Irish Pavilion at the 53rd Venice Biennale. Collection Kildare County Council

Installation views at *IrelandVenice*, Istituto Santa Maria della Pietà, Venice, 2009 (pages 63, 69) and the Golden Thread Gallery, Belfast, 2010 (page 73)

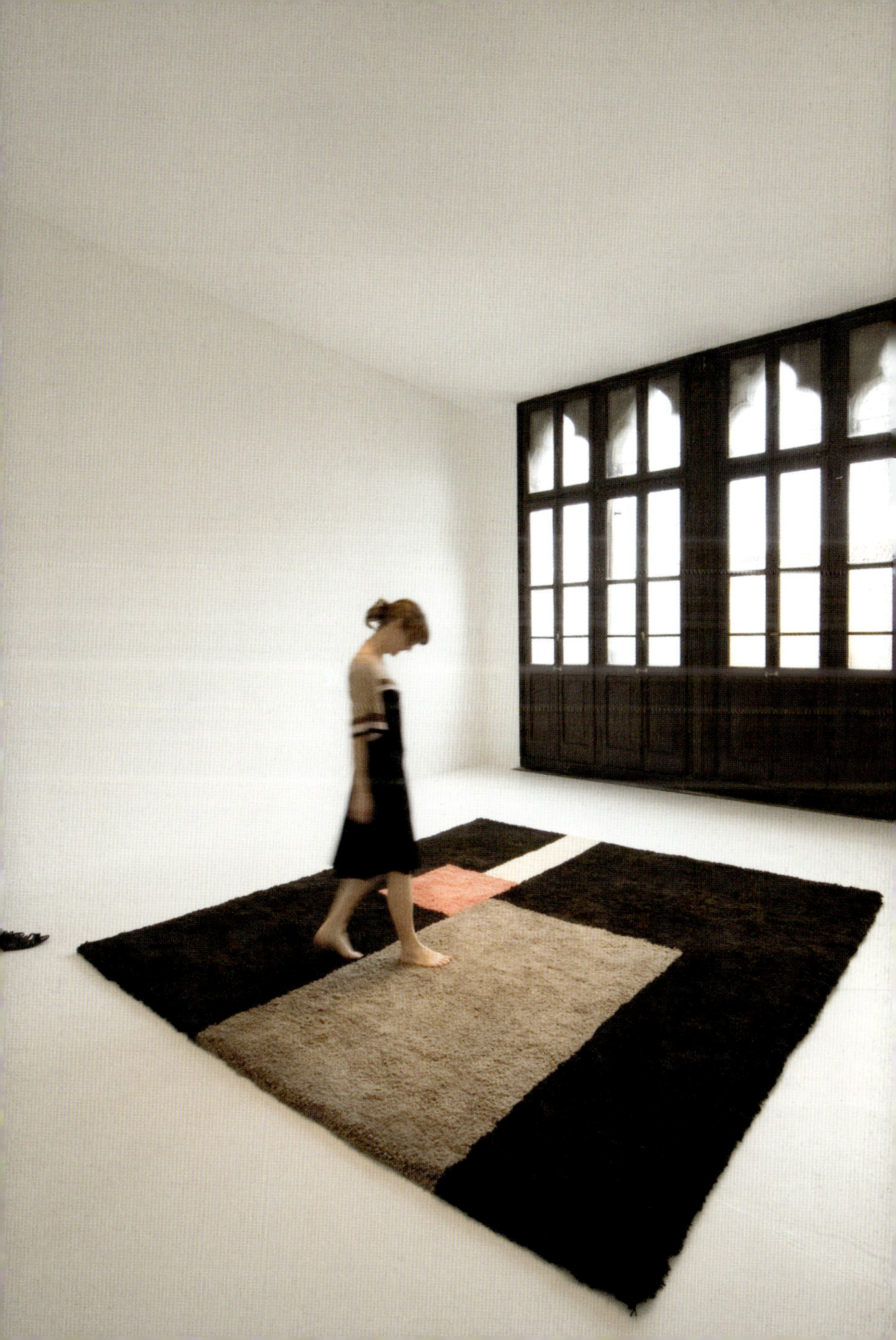

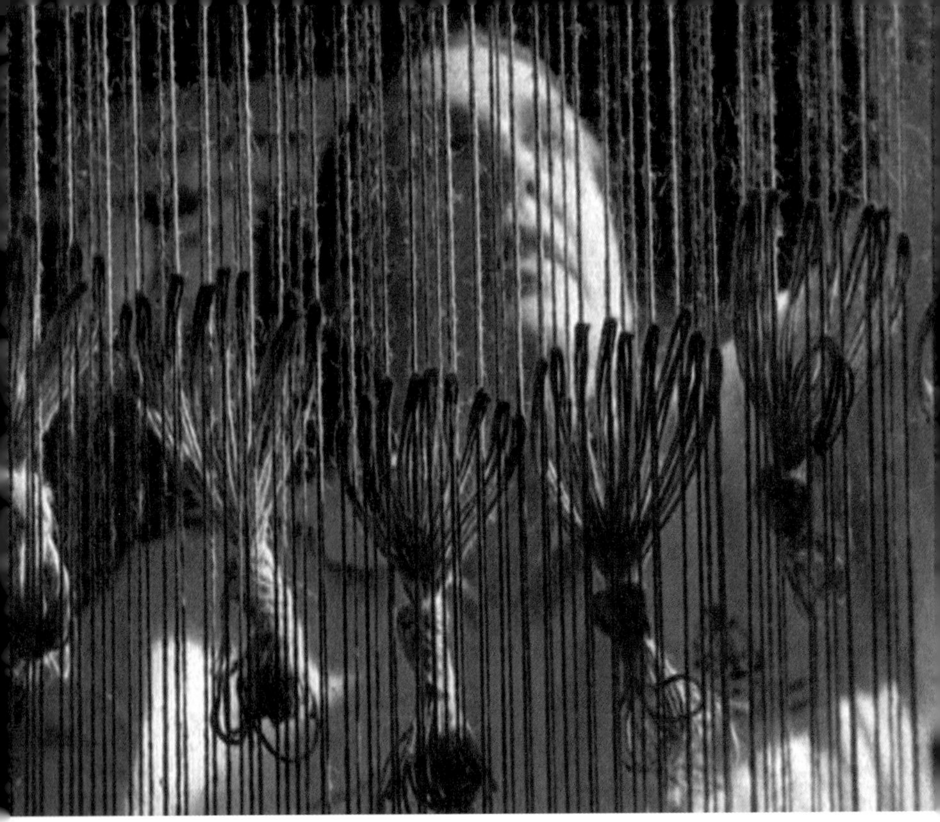

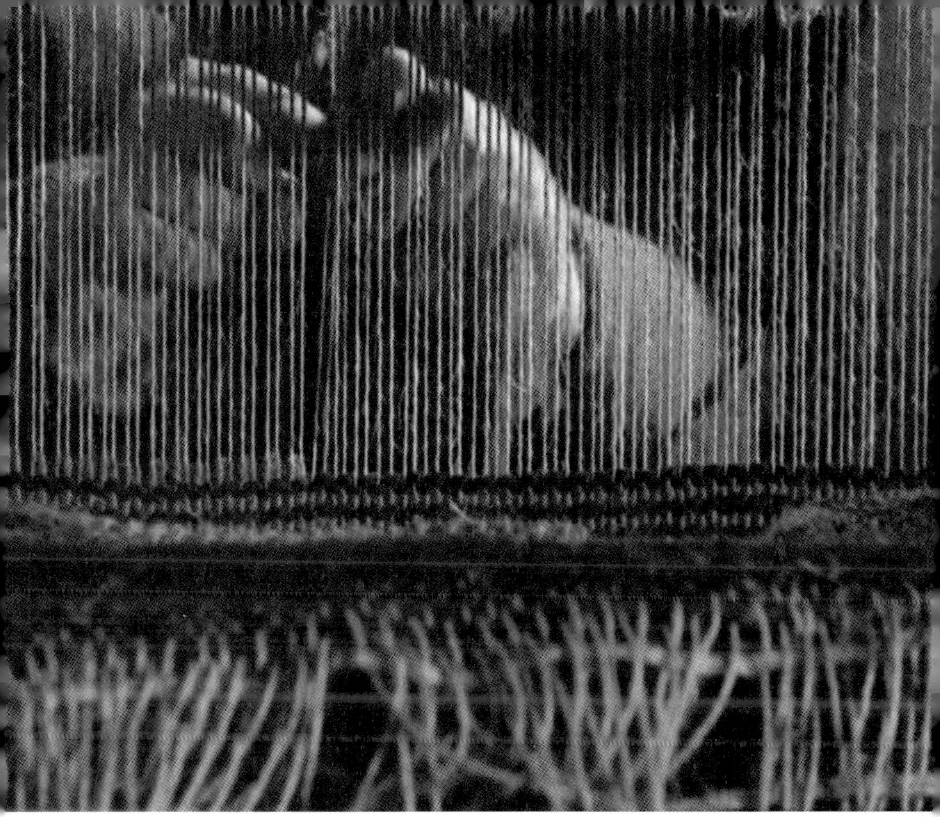

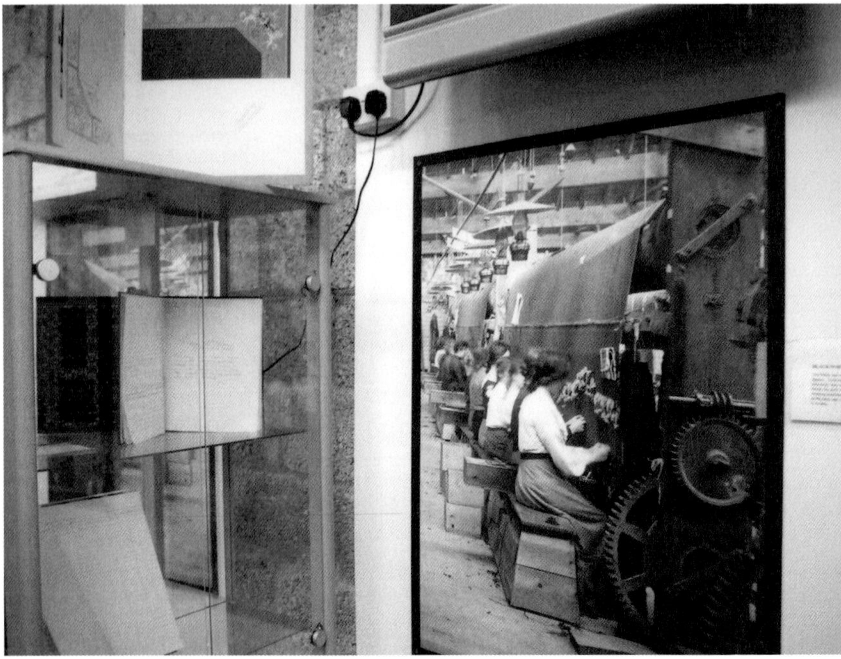

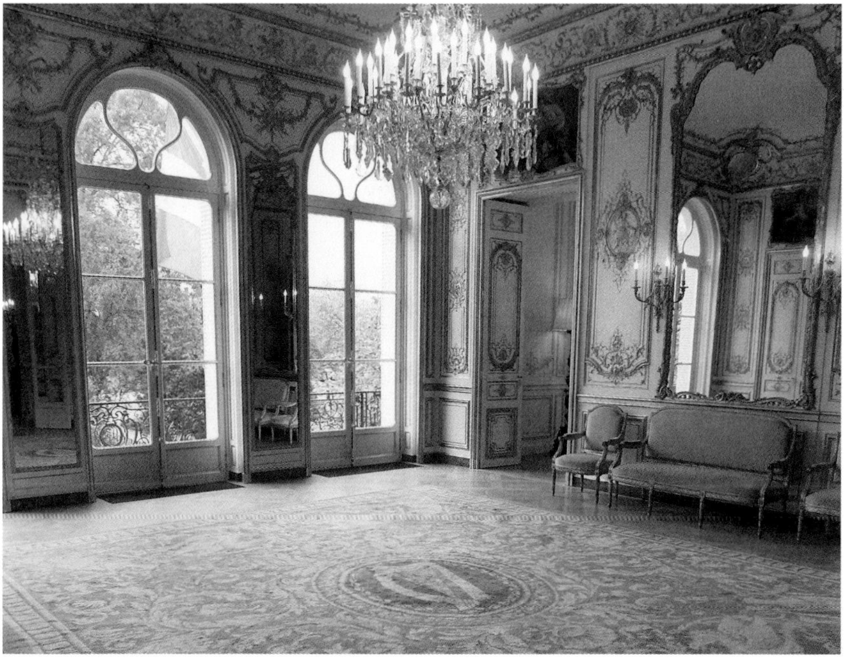

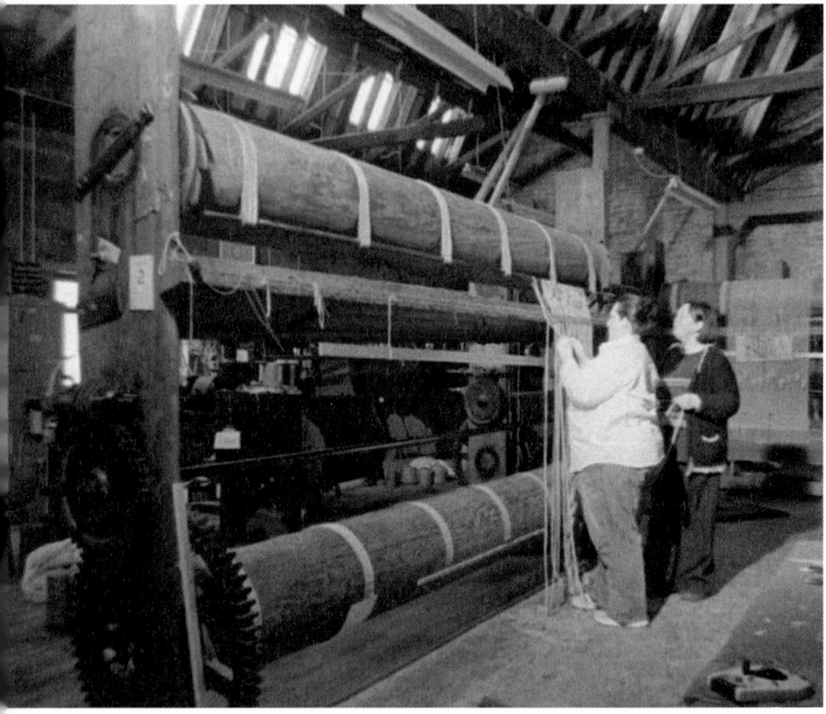

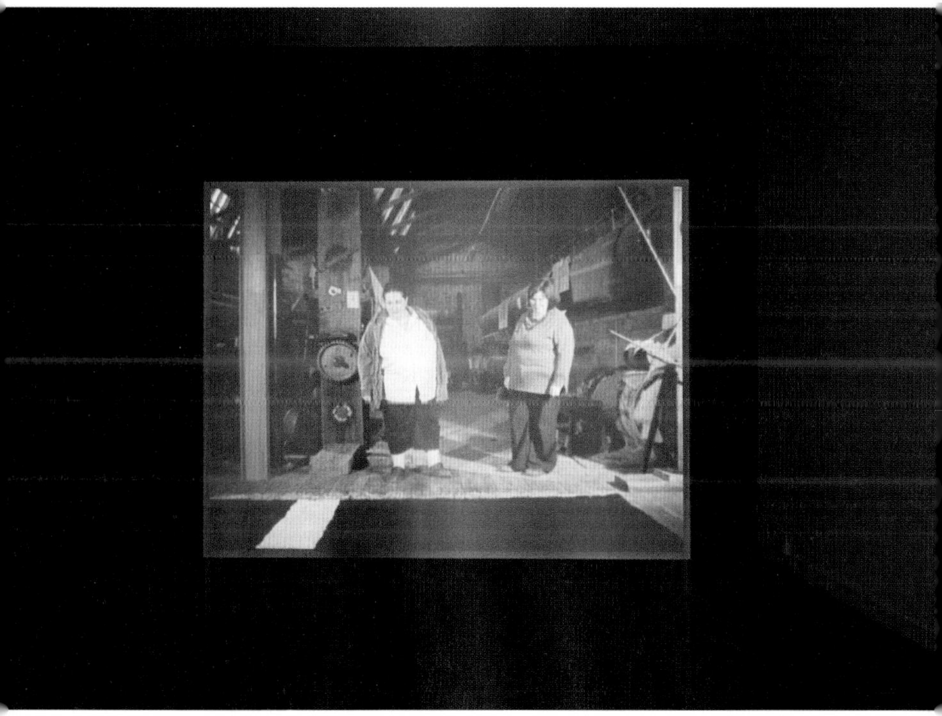

17.16
18.21
1 hour's knotting in one hour's drawing [9 knots per square inch] 1:1
SB 2009

1 hour's knotting in one hour's drawing
[16 knots per square inch]
1:1
SB2019

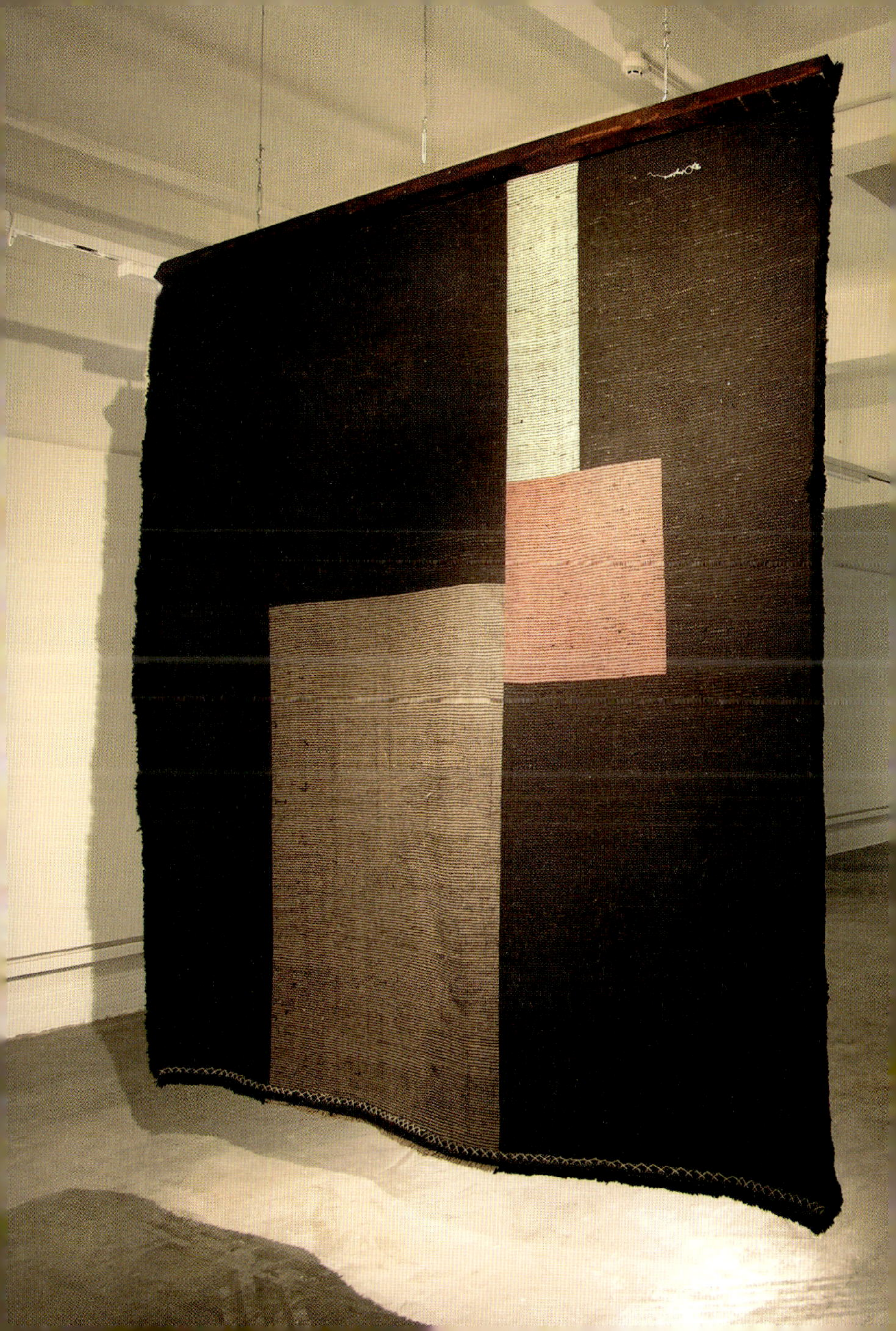

Doorstops for the Daimler Art Collection, 2010
Scale drawing of artist's hand: steel doorstops
Pencil on graph paper, 220mm x 164mm
Collection of the artist

Doorstops for the Daimler Art Collection, 2010
Set of 3 unique doorstops. Cut, milled and polished solid stainless steel
60mm x 136mm x 26mm; 46mm x 155mm x 26mm;
30mm x 160mm x 30mm

Exhibited with *From Margin to Margin (Looking for Eileen)*, 2010
46 page folding leperello, 736cm when fully extended, edition of 200
Proceeds from the sale of the book to be used in the service of the memory of Eileen Gray

Both works commissioned by the Daimler Art Collection
Installation views at *Minimalism and Applied II*, Daimler Contemporary, Berlin, 2010

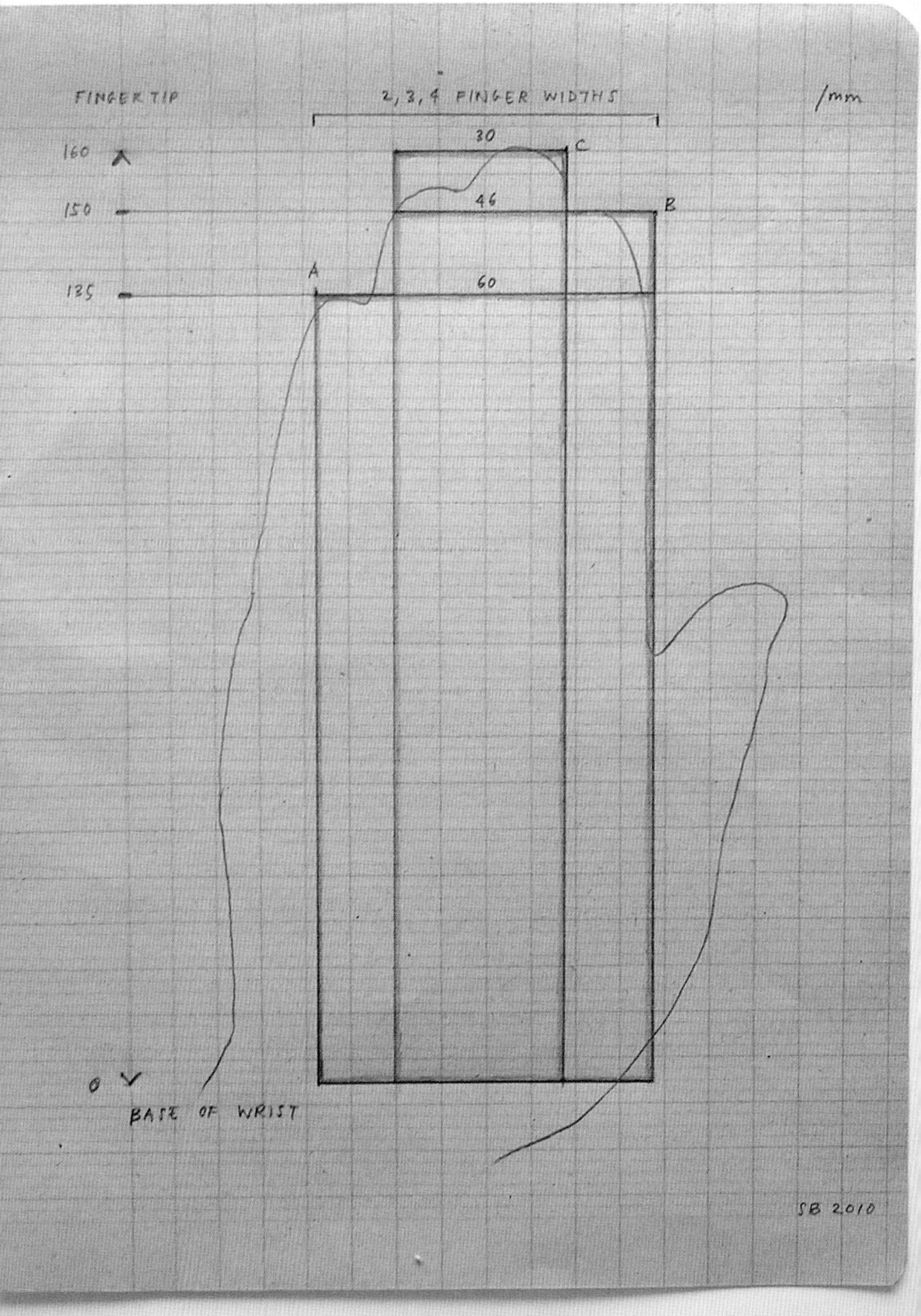
FINGER TIP
2, 3, 4 FINGER WIDTHS
/mm
30
C
160
46
B
150
A
60
135
0
BASE OF WRIST
SB 2010

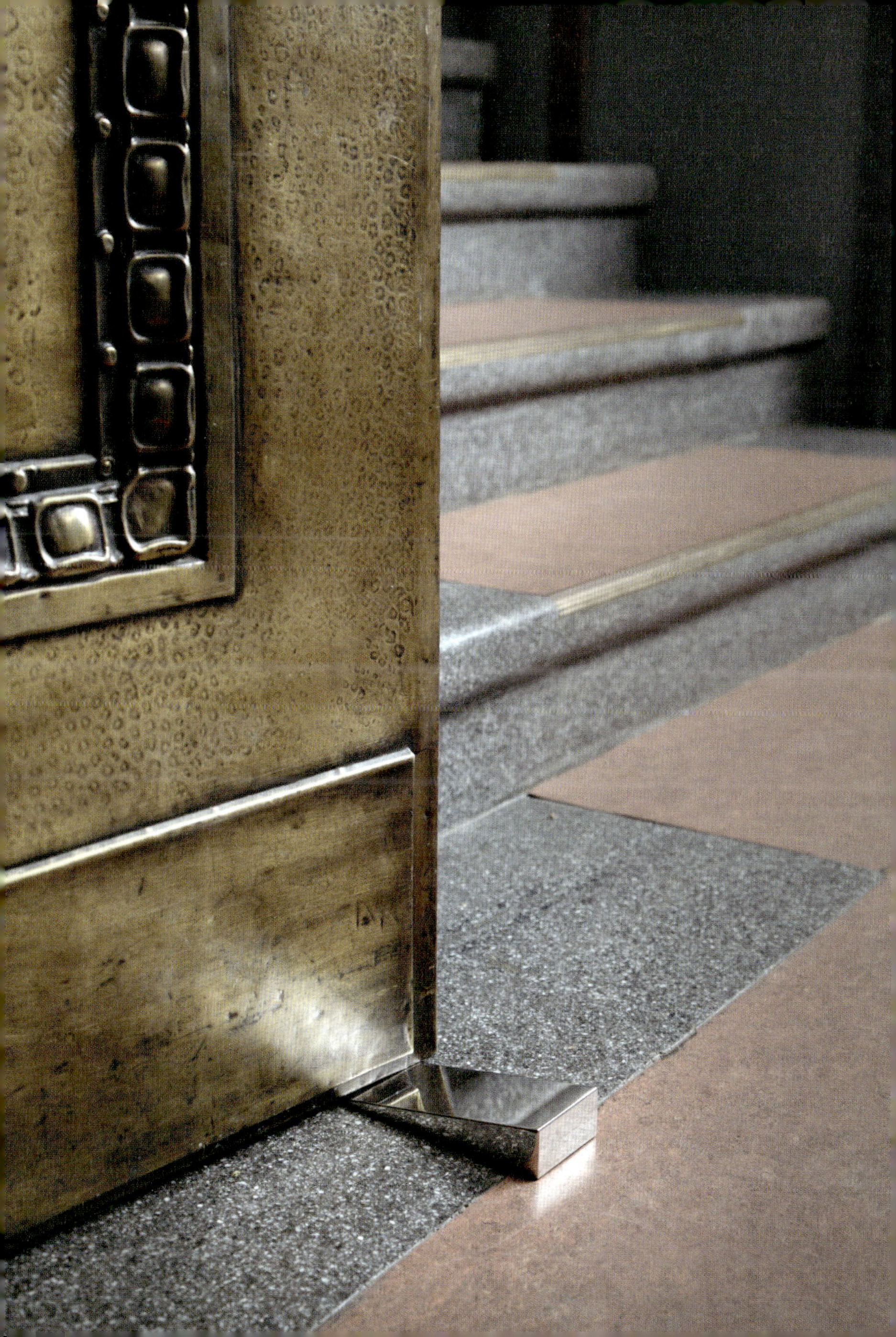

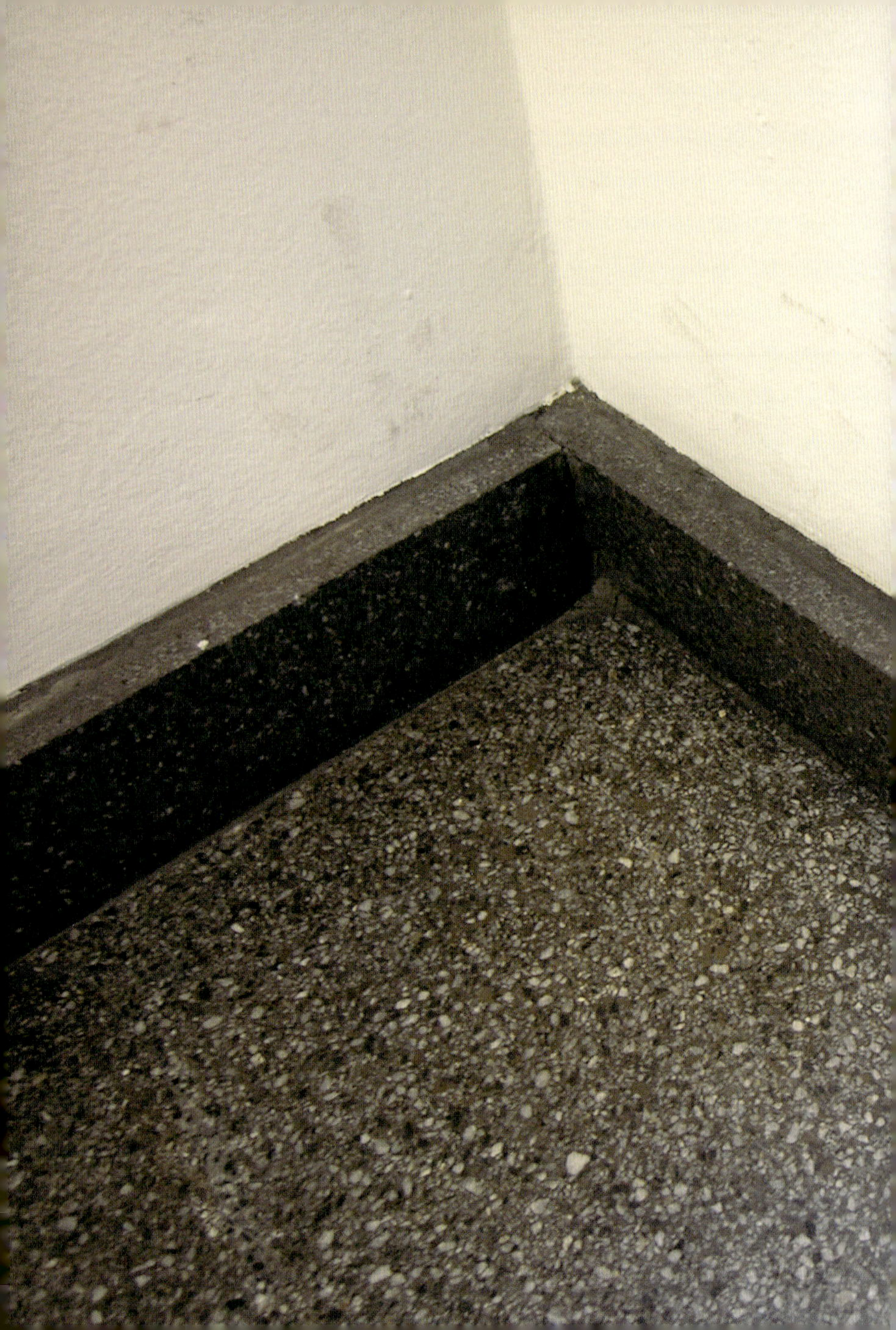

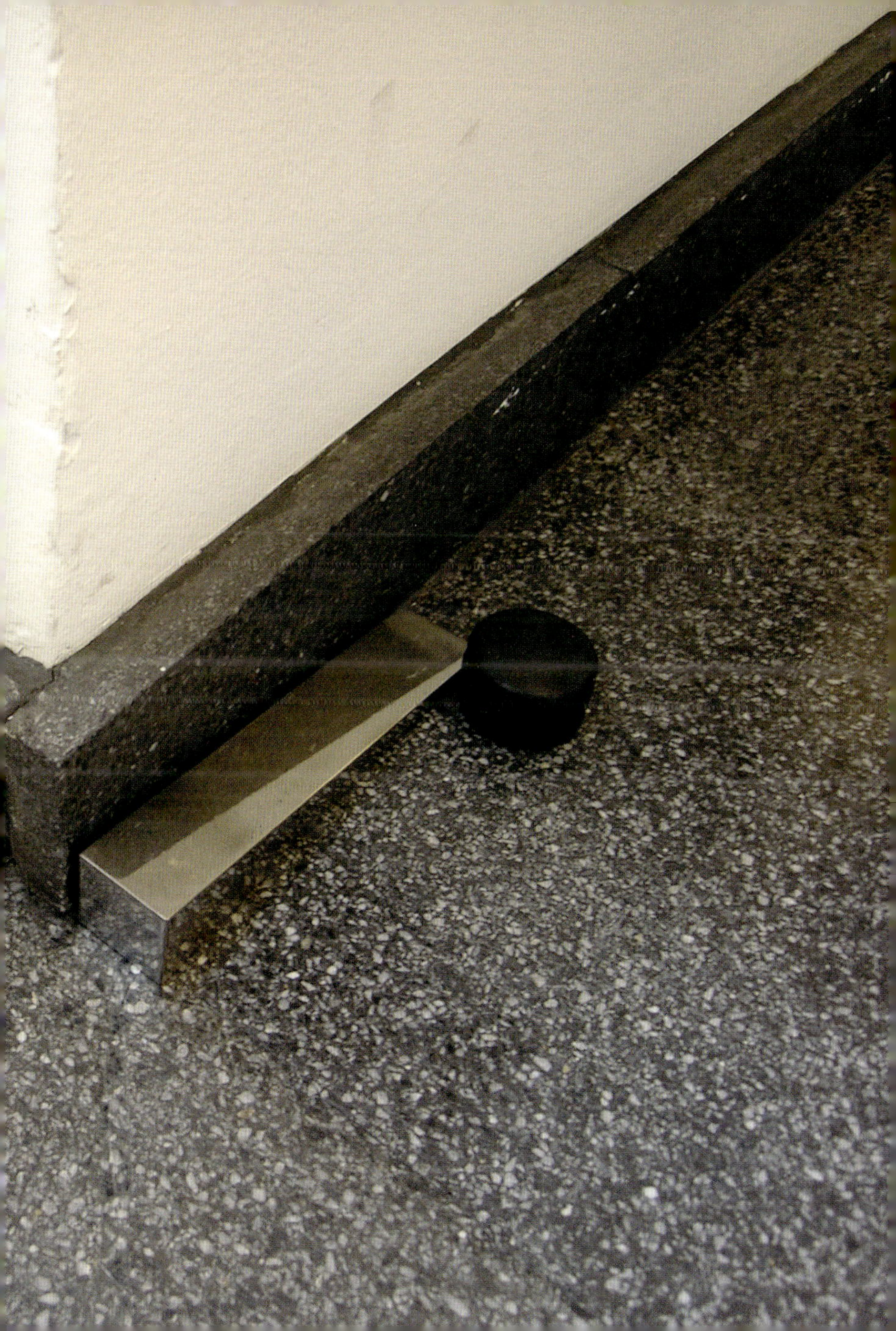

On Hoarding, Accumulating and Gifting / L'Amas, l'Accumulation et le Don, 2011
16 page newspaper in French and English, 265mm x 410mm, b/w
First edition of 1500 published by Project Press, Dublin ISBN 978 1 872493 32 9
Distributed in Le Blanc and in Dublin at the solo exhibition *Second Burial at Le Blanc*, Project Arts Centre 6th May – 23rd June 2011
(Adapted single-language version reproduced here)

L'AMAS, L'ACCUMULATION ET LE DON

ON HOARDING, ACCUMULATING AND GIFTING

This newspaper distributes a visual essay in preparation for shooting a film at Le Blanc, Indre, France on 1st April 2011.

This film fuses the traditions of salvage ethnography (the documentation of dying customs and rituals) with surrealist ethnography (attempting to make the familiar and everyday seem strange). With the participation of local shopkeepers and residents, a procession is being staged from the modern Hôtel de Ville in the main square to Château Naillac, the medieval castle that overlooks the village on the far side of the river and houses a small museum. The object being carried by the procession is a customised stock ticker, which both tracks euro currency exchange rates and works as a countdown clock. This clock prints the days, hours, minutes and seconds until 17th February 2012, when French francs will finally pass from use in Le Blanc, ten years after the first introduction of the euro.

This paradoxical object, which accumulates masses of paper as it measures time running out, is intended as a gift to the town, or at least a loan until the end of its useful life. In the light of the ongoing financial crisis in the Eurozone, this small town in France presents a moment where through the use of an obsolete currency, a parallel sense of time exists, perhaps an envelope of *déjà vu.* Although the passing of the franc is a foregone conclusion, the situation in Le Blanc allows us a window to look forwards into a past that has already happened. The staged ritual around this clock-monument asks - knowing what we know now, should next year's funeral be in the spirit of mourning, or celebration?

Le Blanc is the last village in France where francs are still being accepted as payment for goods and services, although technically the currency is no longer legal tender. A coalition of local artisans and shopkeepers, the Art'Com'In (Artisanat Commerce Industrie Le Blanc), started a scheme in 2007 in order to attract people to the region and boost the local economy. The Association is clear that the scheme was not introduced through any social or political resistance to the euro, or any particular attachment to the franc, emotional or ideological. The francs accepted by participating shopkeepers are collected and exchanged at the Banque de France in Limoges, with traders reimbursed in euros. This will continue until next year, when the town hopes to have collected 2 million francs (€300,000). Le Blanc is not unique in Europe however: as of 3rd March 2011, a fishing village called Mugardos in northern Spain has decided to reintroduce the old currency – the peseta – alongside the euro in a bid to encourage purchases in times of severe recession.

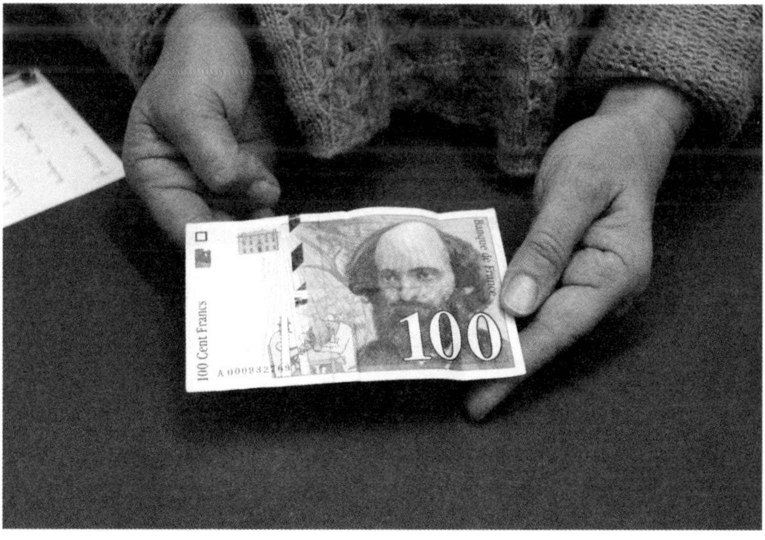

January 28th 2011, Sylvie Auteau presents a 100 Franc note collected at her shop in Le Blanc.

Nobody ever told the proverbial man in the street that sharing a single currency was not just about making peoples' lives easier when doing business or travelling abroad, but also about being directly affected by economic developments in the neighbouring countries. Today, people are discovering what a 'common destiny' in monetary matters means. They are discovering that the euro affects their pensions, savings, and jobs, their very daily life. It hurts.

—Herman Van Rompuy, President of the European Council,
The Daily Telegraph, London, 26th May 2010

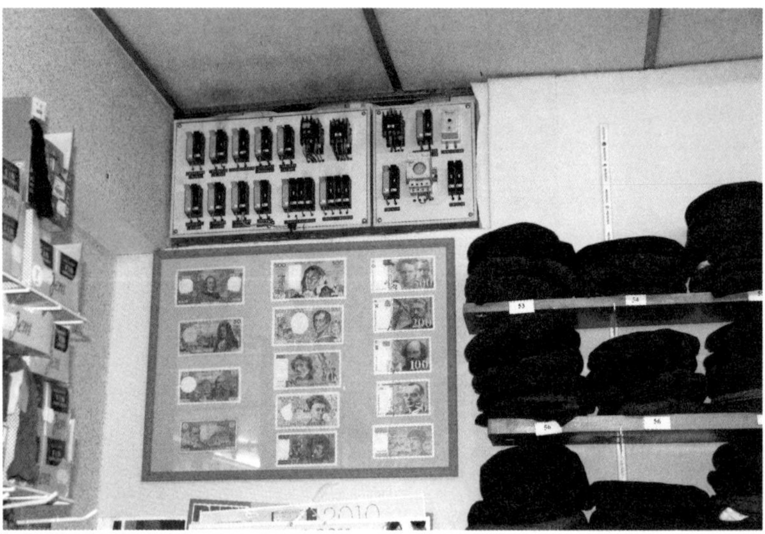

Display of selection of French franc banknotes, Moenne Loccoz, Rue de Souvigny, Le Blanc, January 2011.

On establishment of the Eurozone in 1999, the central bank in each member nation determined the final date for when its currency would no longer be exchangeable for euros. In France, the Banque de France marked 17th February 2012 as this final deadline.

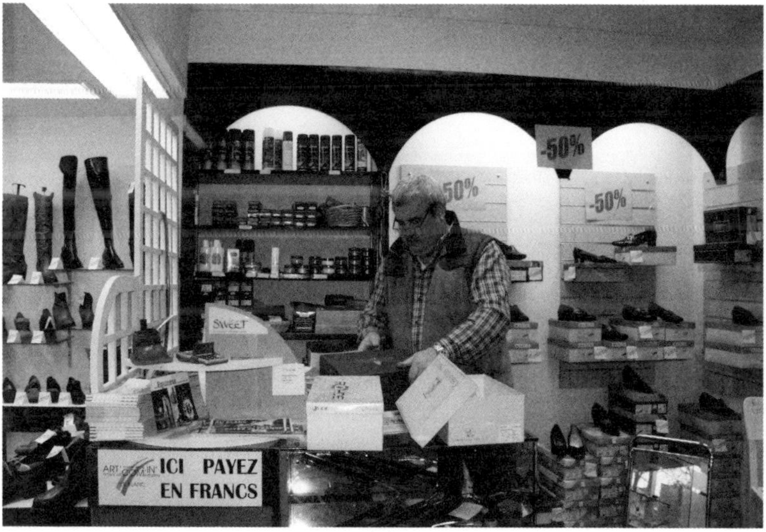

M. Pruvost serving a customer at Chaussures Pruvost, Place André Gasnier, Le Blanc, January 2011.
(below) Countdown clock to the last days of the franc on the website of the Art'Com'In' www.artcomin.fr

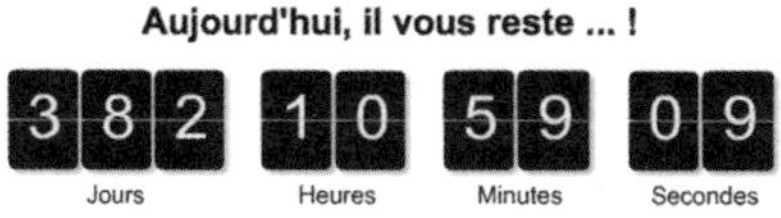

It's not clear if people coming to spend their francs at Le Blanc have saved up large quantities over time, or not. Certainly, many francs are found in the pockets of old jackets and between the pages of forgotten books. Other francs may have been squirrelled away for years, or inherited in bulk as 'mattress money'. Marx describes the accumulation of money, without the means to transform it into capital, not as capitalist accumulation but as hoarding – a never-ending task.

Sociologists analysing the reluctance of consumers to dispose of material possessions and to accumulate obsolete items define this as behaviour that 'reflects a desire to reassemble the fragments of their temporal experience into a unique space, where memories, present, and life projects join together.'

—Hélène Cherrier, Tresa Ponnor, 'A study of hoarding behavior and attachment to material possessions,' *Qualitative Market Research: An International Journal*, Vol. 13 Issue 1, 2010

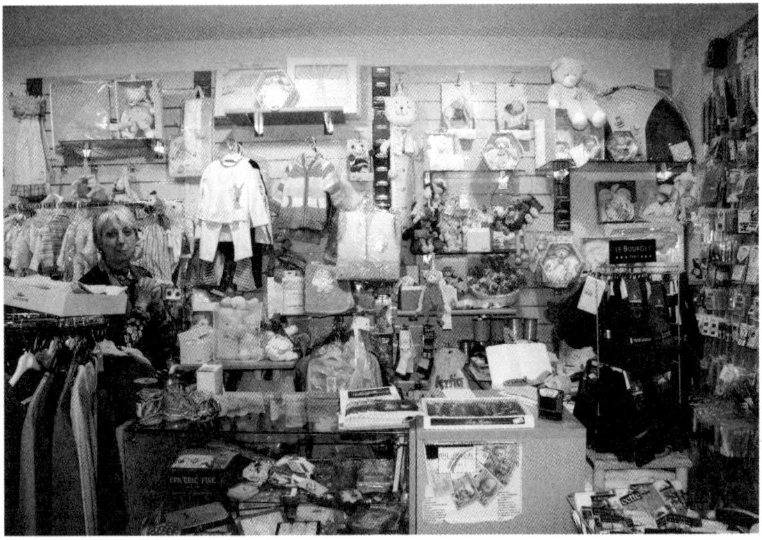

Artifil, Rue du General LeClerc, Le Blanc, 2011.

A currency that became obsolete around forty years ago, *Rai* stones are made from limestone. This material is not indigenous to Yap, but quarried and shipped, primarily from the islands of Palau, 250 miles to the southwest. The stones are not known to have any particular use other than as a representation of value. They were not functional, nor were they spiritually significant to their owners; and by most accounts, the stones have no obvious ornamental value to the Yapese either. Precisely how the value of each stone was determined is also somewhat unclear; size was at best only a rough approximation of worth. Stone values varied depending upon the cost or difficulty of bringing them to the island: those gotten at great peril, perhaps even loss of life, were valued most highly. *Rai* was in use as currency until the 1960s and maintained purchasing power reasonably well over time (particularly compared with other fiat monies, including dollars).

> *In the West as in the Rest, rationality is an expression of the culture, of its meaningful system of utilities... To understand our economy requires the same kind of anthropological sensibility we bring to the study of others. We are one of the others.*
>
> —Marshall Sahlins, preface to the new edition (2003) of *Stone Age Economics*, Routledge, London, 1972

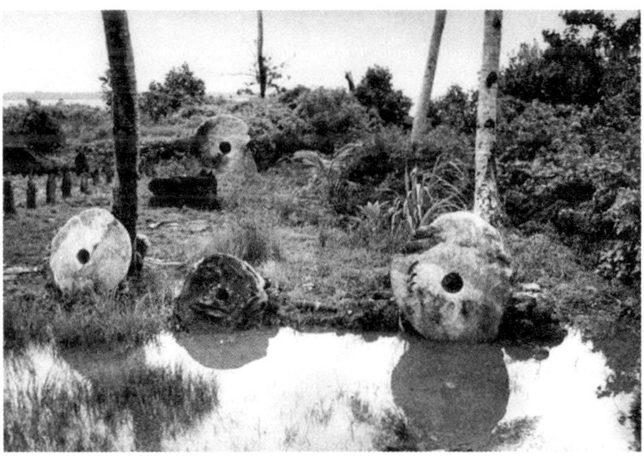

Stone money from the island of Yap, Caroline Islands, Pacific Ocean, 2009.

In comparison to the 120-step-per-minute pace of other French units, the Legion has an 88-step-per-minute marching speed. Referred to by Legionnaires as the 'crawl', it can be seen at ceremonial parades and public displays attended by the Legion, particularly while parading in Paris on the 14th July Bastille Day Parade. Contrary to popular belief, the adoption of the Legion's slow marching speed was not due to a need to preserve energy and fluids during long marches under the hot Algerian sun. Its exact origins are somewhat unclear. The official explanation is that although the pace regulation does not seem to have been instituted before 1945, it hails back to the slow, majestic marching pace of the *Ancien Régime*. Its reintroduction is explained as a 'return to traditional roots'.

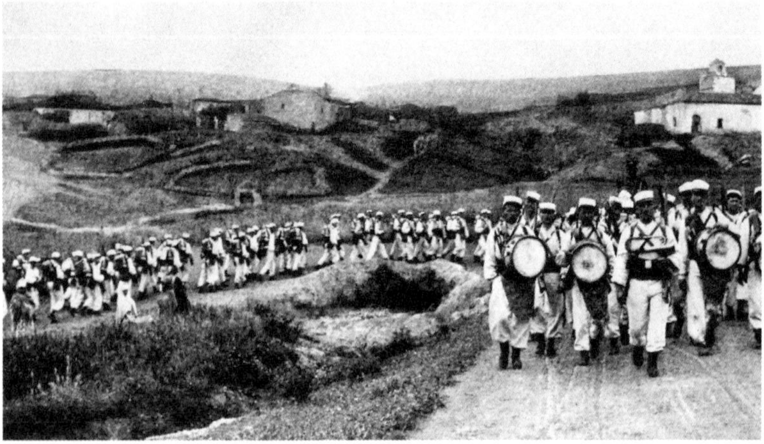

The Slow March of the French Foreign Legion, Algeria, late 1800s.

A first burial is sometimes followed by a second burial, the period of waiting often coinciding with the duration of decomposition. In Madagascar, a family will dig up their dead ancestors at the appropriate spiritual time and parade the deceased around the village, showing them the new developments, all the while talking to them as though they were alive. Then they clean the departed's bones and wrap them carefully in a fresh shroud (*lamba mena*) for re-burial. The old shroud is presented to a recently married couple in the family to make love on, in the belief that the ancestor's worth will inhabit any resulting offspring. The family of the departed prepares a feast following the re-burial for the hundreds of people who attend, a gift that often bankrupts the family.

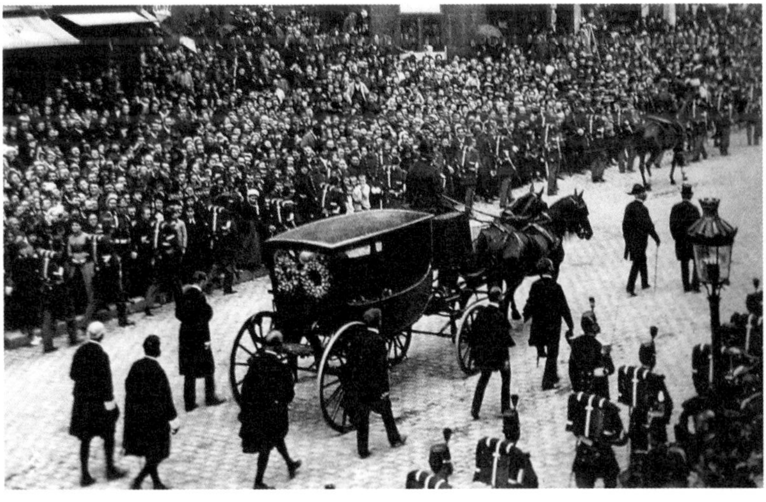

Interment of Victor Hugo, en route to the Pantheon, Paris, 1st June 1885.

The Statue of Liberty Enlightening the World was an international gift of friendship from the people of France to the people of the United States, dedicated in 1886. Historian Maurice Agulhon observes a democratic mass production of public monuments during this time in France, which he described as 'statuomania', identifying it as an important precursor to local memorials after World War I. Other strategies of the Third Republic to blend state pomp with citizen celebration included the invention of public ceremonies such as Bastille Day, the first of which can be dated to 1880.

> *The gift: the present generously given even when, in the gesture accompanying the transaction, there is only a polite fiction, formalism, and social deceit, and when really there is obligation and economic self-interest… what rule of legality and self-interest, in societies of a backward or archaic type, compels the gift that has been received to be obligatorily reciprocated? What is the power that resides in the object that causes the recipient to pay it back?*
>
> —Marcel Mauss, *The Gift* (trans.), 1954

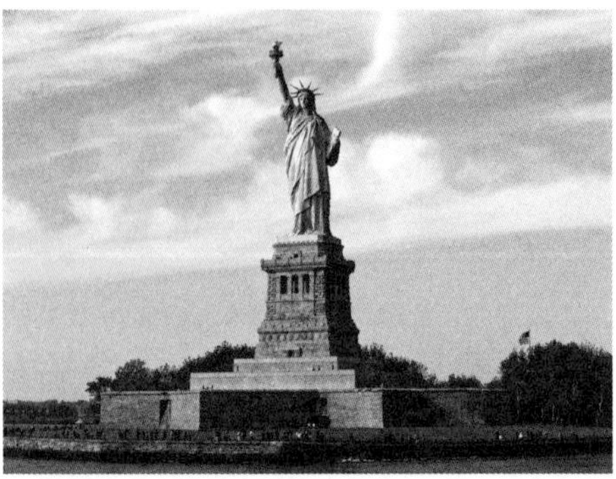

The Statue of Liberty, New York, 2008.

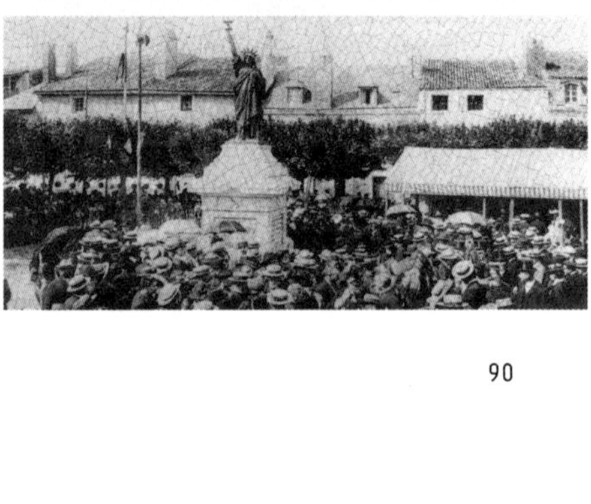

Inauguration of a replica in Poitiers, 1903.

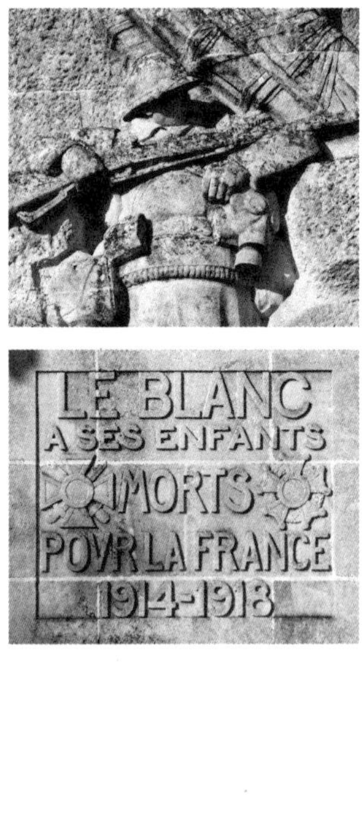

World War I memorial, Place de Liberation, Le Blanc.

The first ticker tape parade was in New York City after a spontaneous celebration held on 28th October 1886 during the dedication of the Statue of Liberty. Ticker tape was thrown from the windows of the offices in the Financial District as the procession below, beginning in Madison Square, passed to Broadway. Soon after this first parade, city officials realised the utility of such events and began to organise them on triumphal occasions – an unofficial, impulsive celebration became the basis for an officially invented tradition. Following World War II, several ticker tape parades were given in honour of victorious generals and admirals. Through the 1950s, ticker-tape parades were commonly given to any visiting head of state, but became increasingly rare in the 1960s following the assassination of John F. Kennedy. They are now generally reserved for space exploration triumphs, military honours and sports championships, and the paper products are largely waste office paper that has been cut using conventional paper shredders.

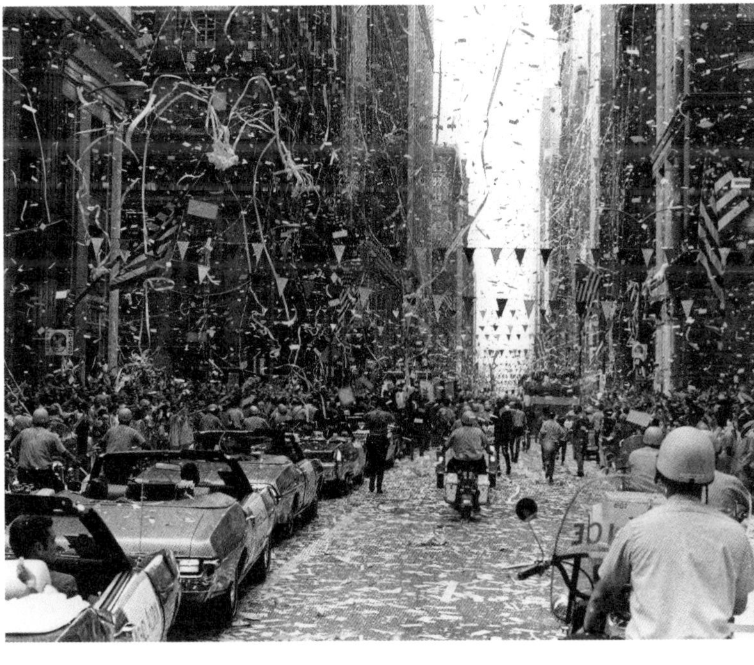

Ticker tape parade in Chicago to celebrate the successful Apollo 11 moon landings, July 1969. Photo by NASA.

Ticker tape was the earliest digital electronic communications medium, transmitting stock price information over telegraph lines, in use from the 1870s until the early 1970s. It consisted of a paper strip running through a machine called a stock ticker, which printed abbreviated company names, followed by numeric stock transaction price and volume information. The term 'ticker tape' came from the sound made by the machine as it printed the thin paper tape. Since the ticker ran continuously, updates to a stock's price whenever the price changed became effective much faster, and trading became a more time sensitive matter. For the first time, trades were being done in what we think of as near real-time. The paper ticker tape started to become obsolete in the 1960s, as television and computers were increasingly used to transmit financial information. The concept of the stock ticker lives on, however, in the scrolling electronic tickers seen on brokerage walls and on financial television networks.

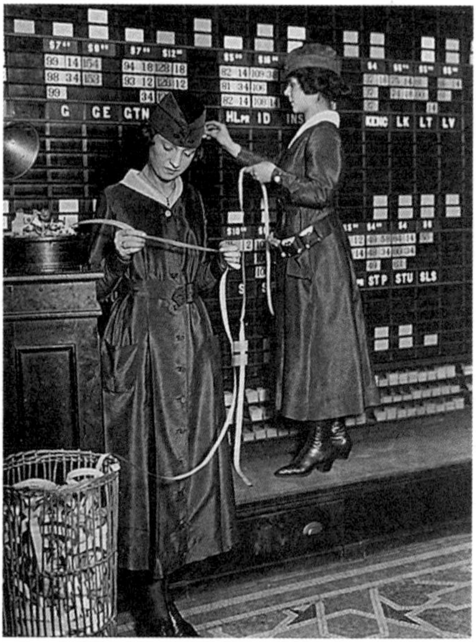

Women operating stock tickers and stock exchange display boards, 11th December 1918.

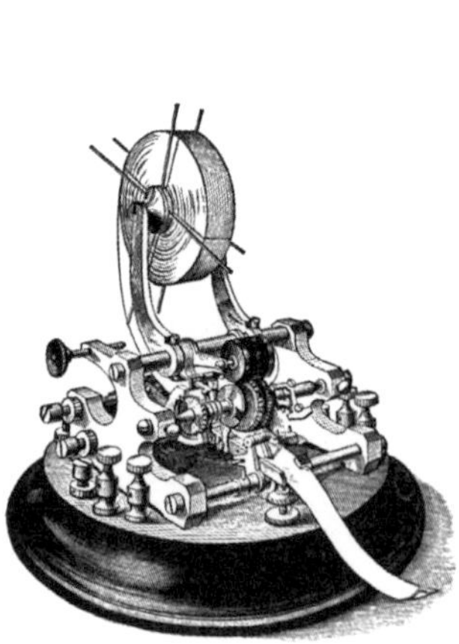

Drawing by William Mayer of the Edison Stock Ticker, invented by Thomas Edison in 1869.

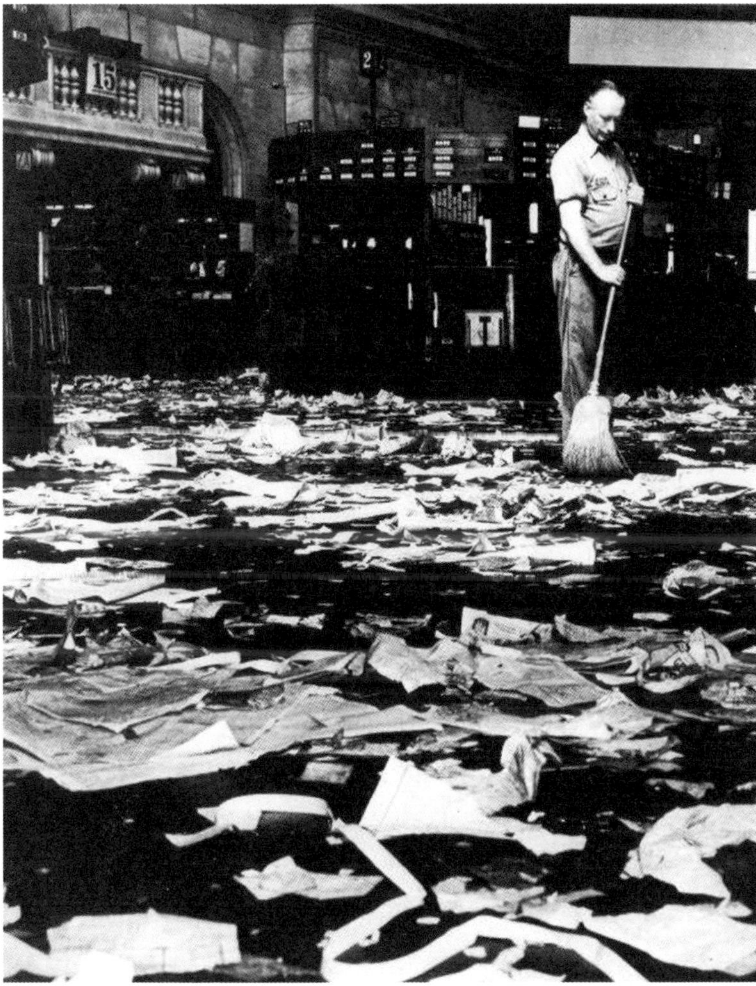

Cleaner sweeping the floor of the New York Stock Exchange on Black Tuesday, 1929. National Archive of the Netherlands, Spaarnestad Collection.

The Doomsday Clock is a symbolic clock face, maintained since 1947 by the board of directors of the *Bulletin of the Atomic Scientists* at the University of Chicago, USA. Counting time with a graph, the numbers on the left refer to the 'minutes to midnight' as the values of the clock are usually expressed. On the right are the raw times. The closer the clock is to midnight, the closer the world is estimated to be to global disaster. Originally, the analogy represented the threat of global nuclear war, but since 2007 it has also reflected climate-changing technologies and new developments in biology and nanotechnology that could inflict irrevocable harm. Since its creation, the time on the clock has changed 19 times. The most recent officially-announced setting – six minutes to midnight – was on 14th January 2010.

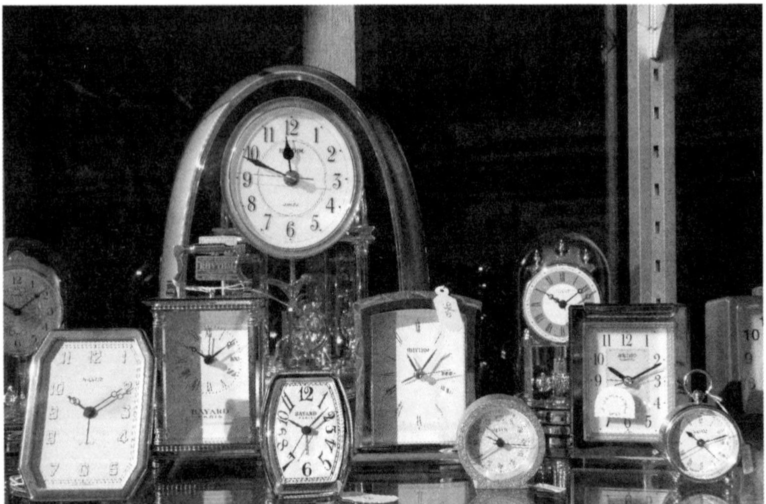

Doomsday Clock of the Bulletin of the Atomic Scientists, Bijouterie Thoreau, Place Andre Gasnier, Le Blanc.

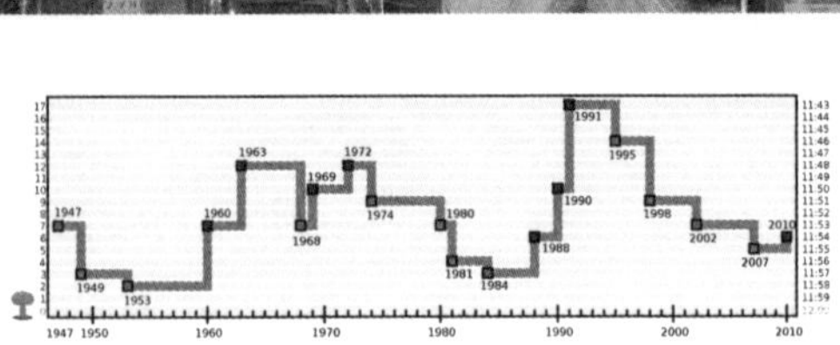

Hyperinflation in the Weimar Republic after World War I rendered much currency worthless. As paper, its use value was greater than its exchange value, and it was put to use for tasks such as wallpapering and lighting fires.

> *The current crisis facing the euro is the biggest test Europe has faced in decades. It is an existential test and it must be overcome… if the euro fails, then Europe fails.*
>
> —Chancellor of Germany, Angela Merkel, 19th May 2010

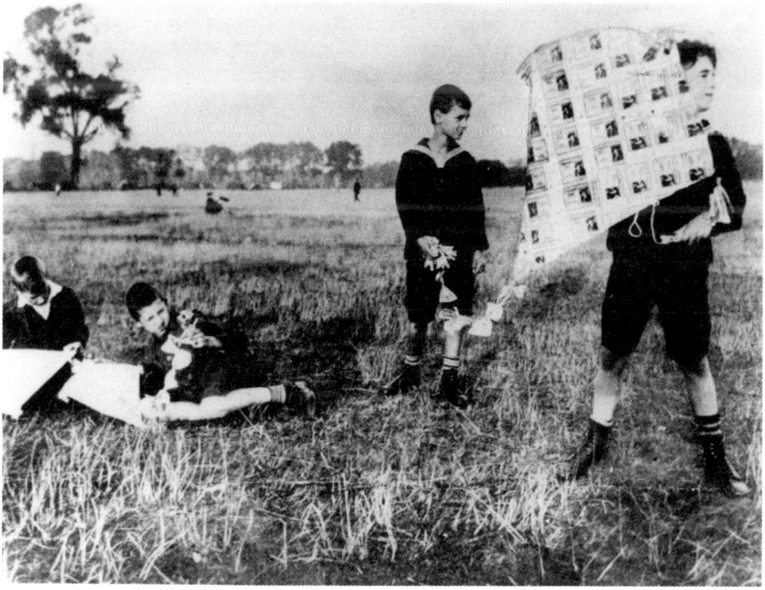

Boy with a kite made of banknotes in Germany, January 1922. Photo by Keystone/Getty Images. Collection of the Hulton Archive.

Second Burial at Le Blanc, 2011
Stills from 16mm film, colour, silent, 8'18"

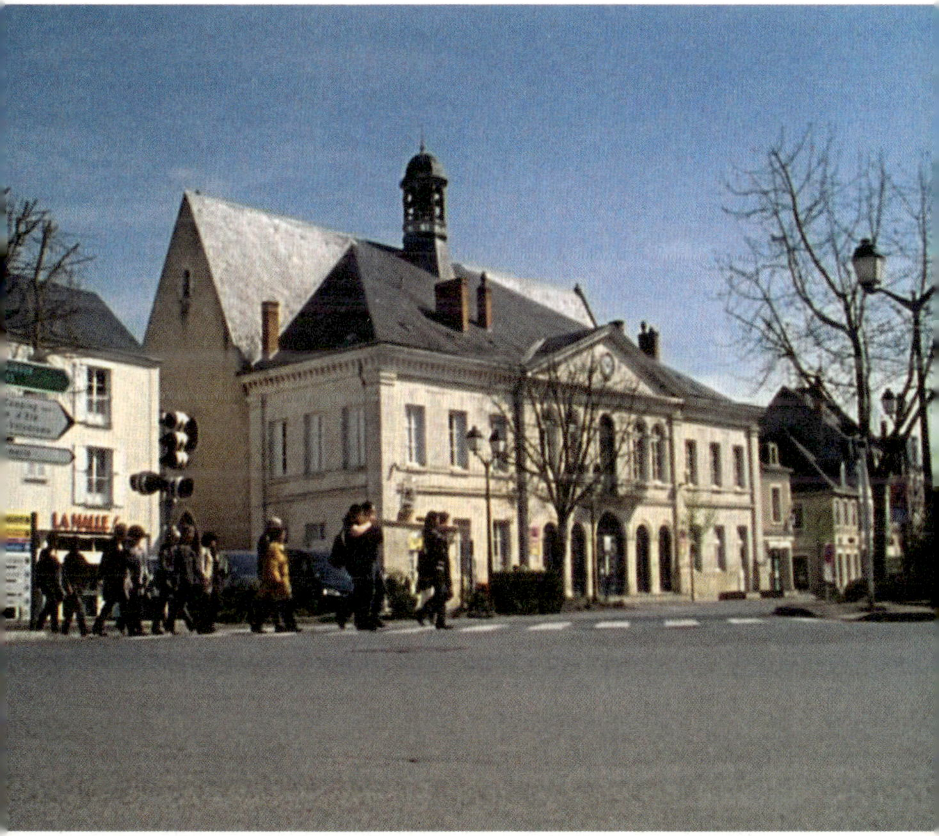
LA HALLE

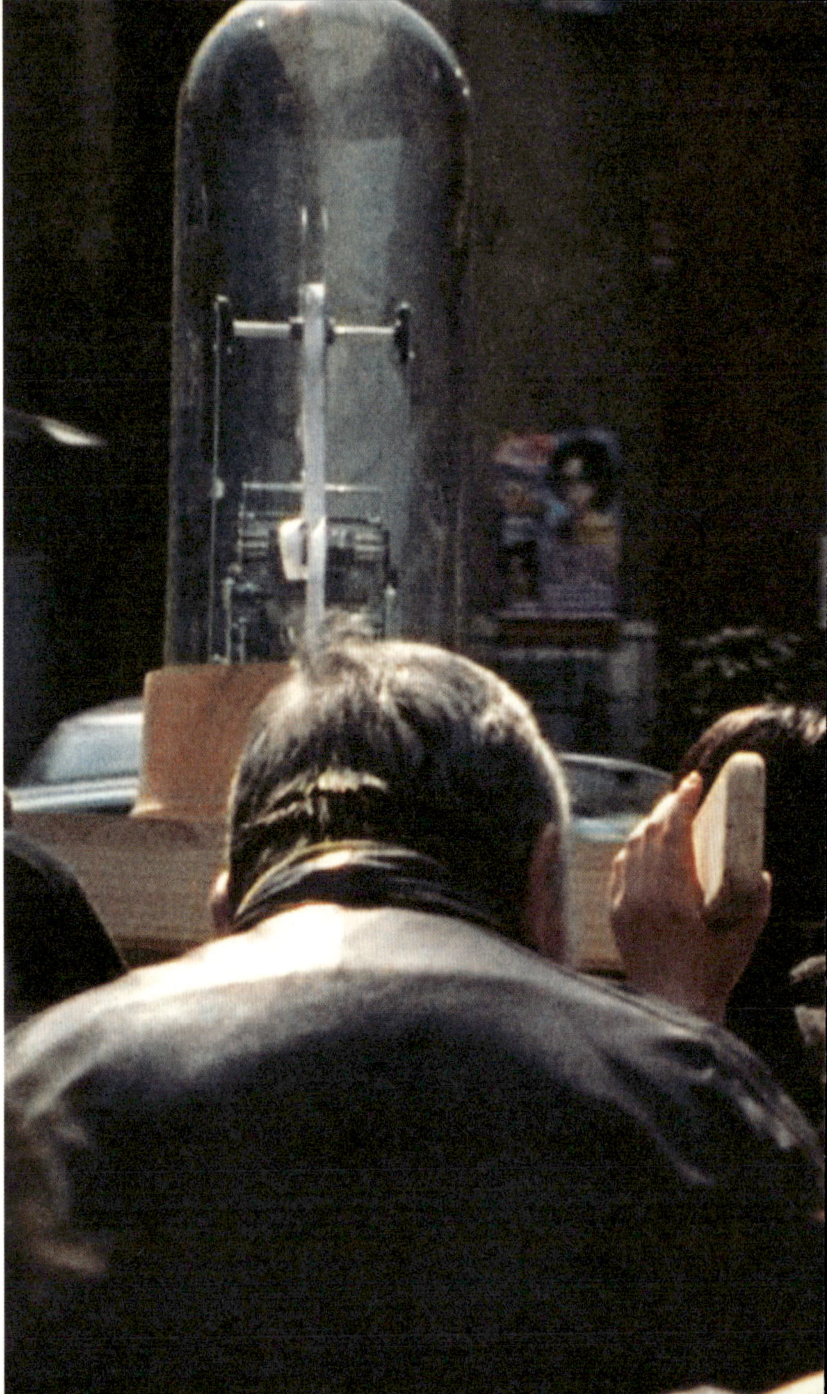

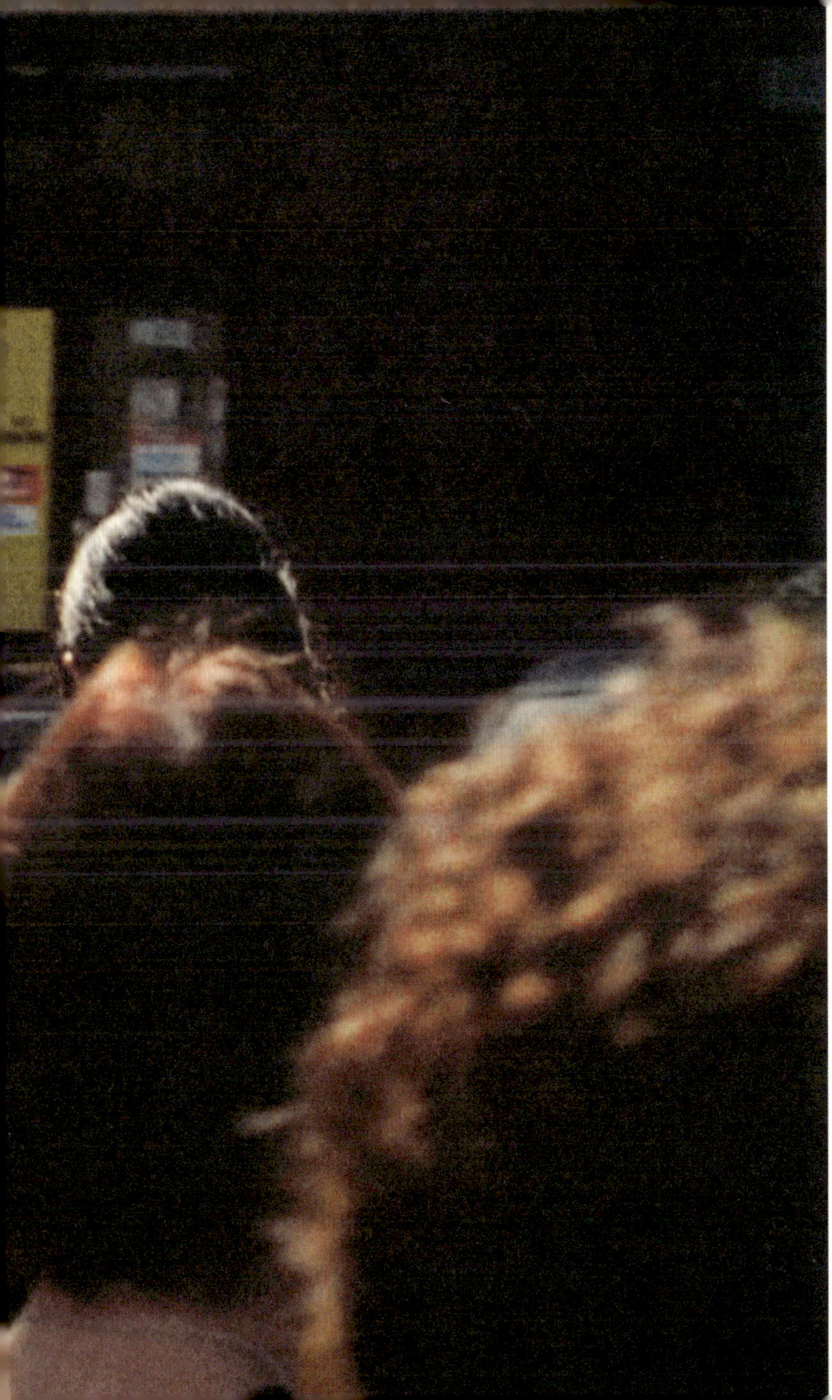

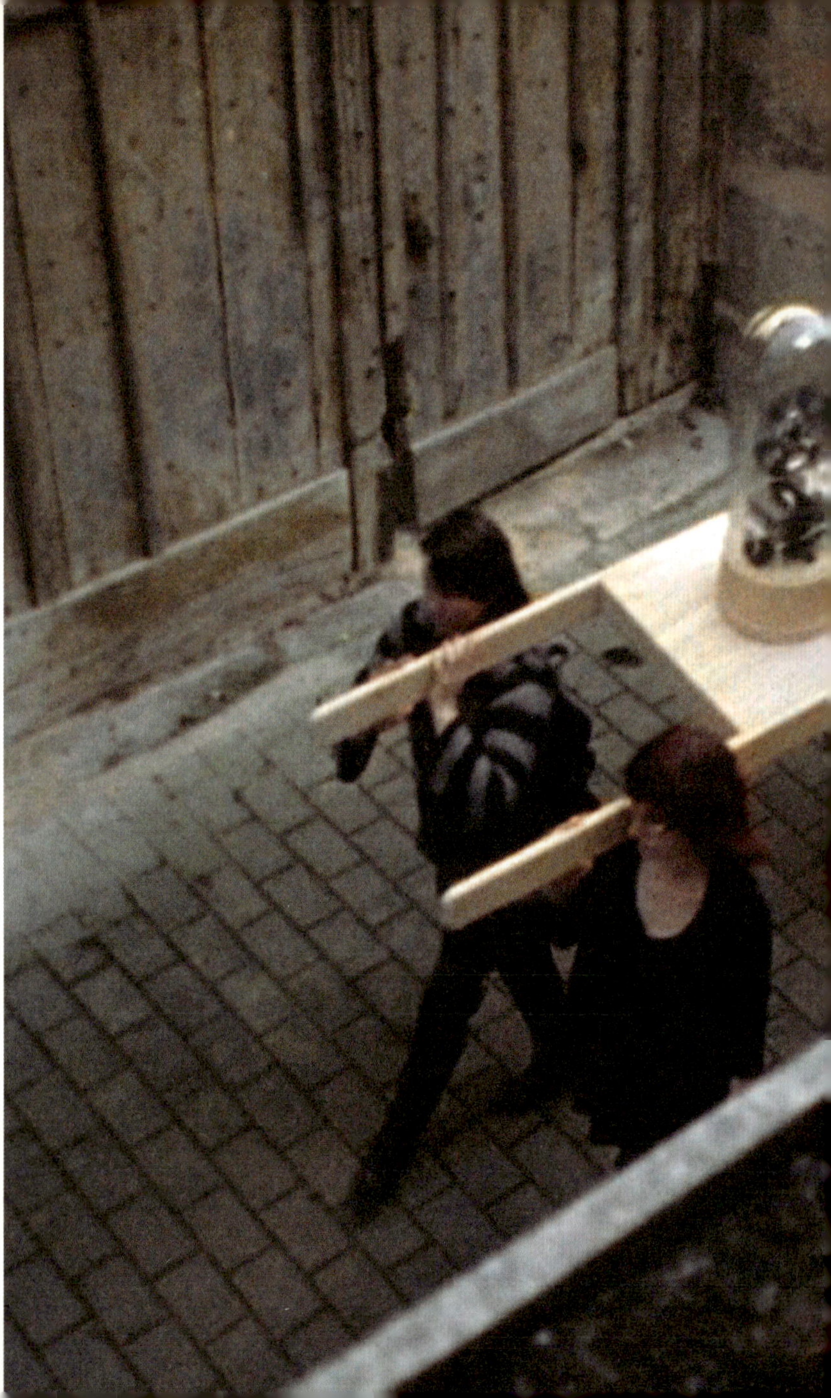

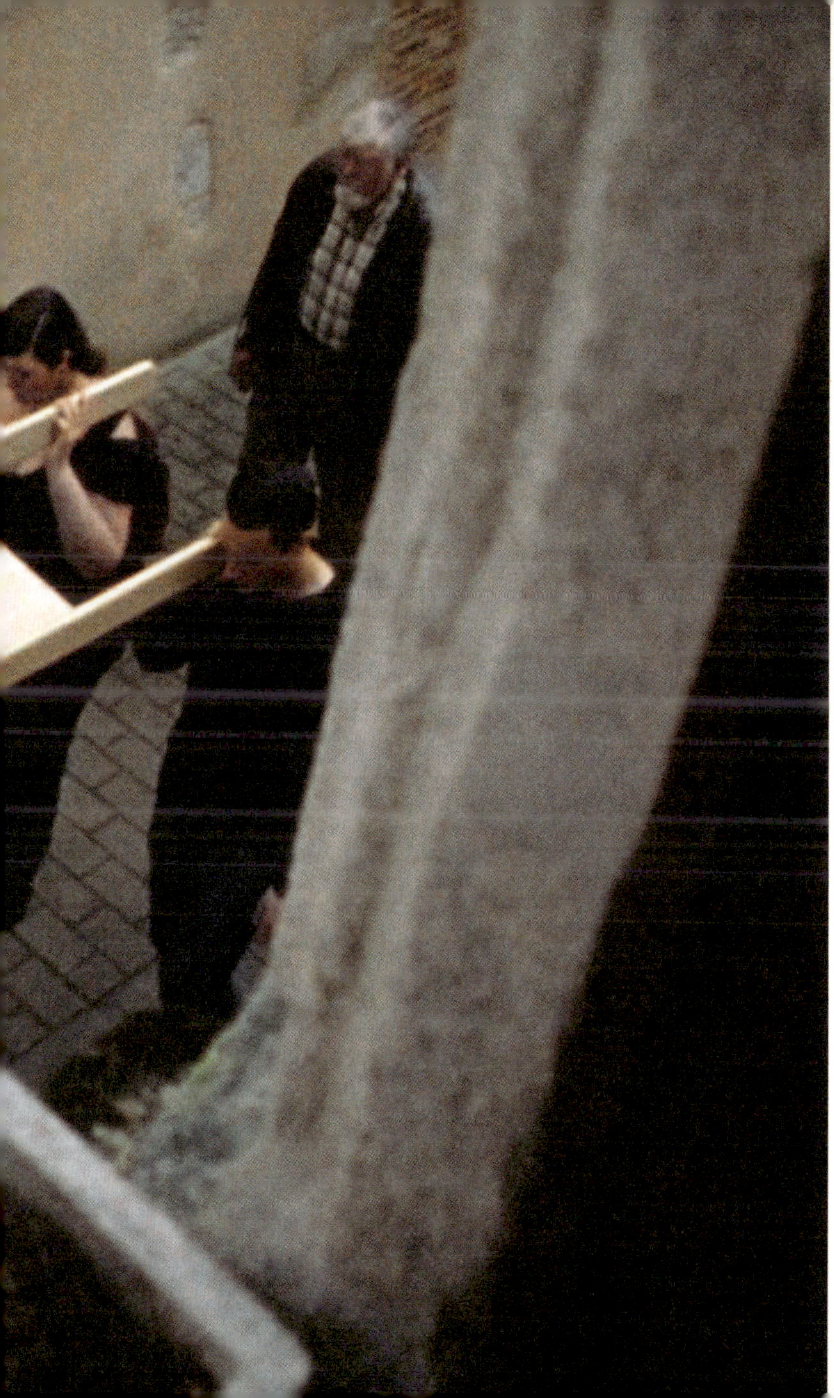

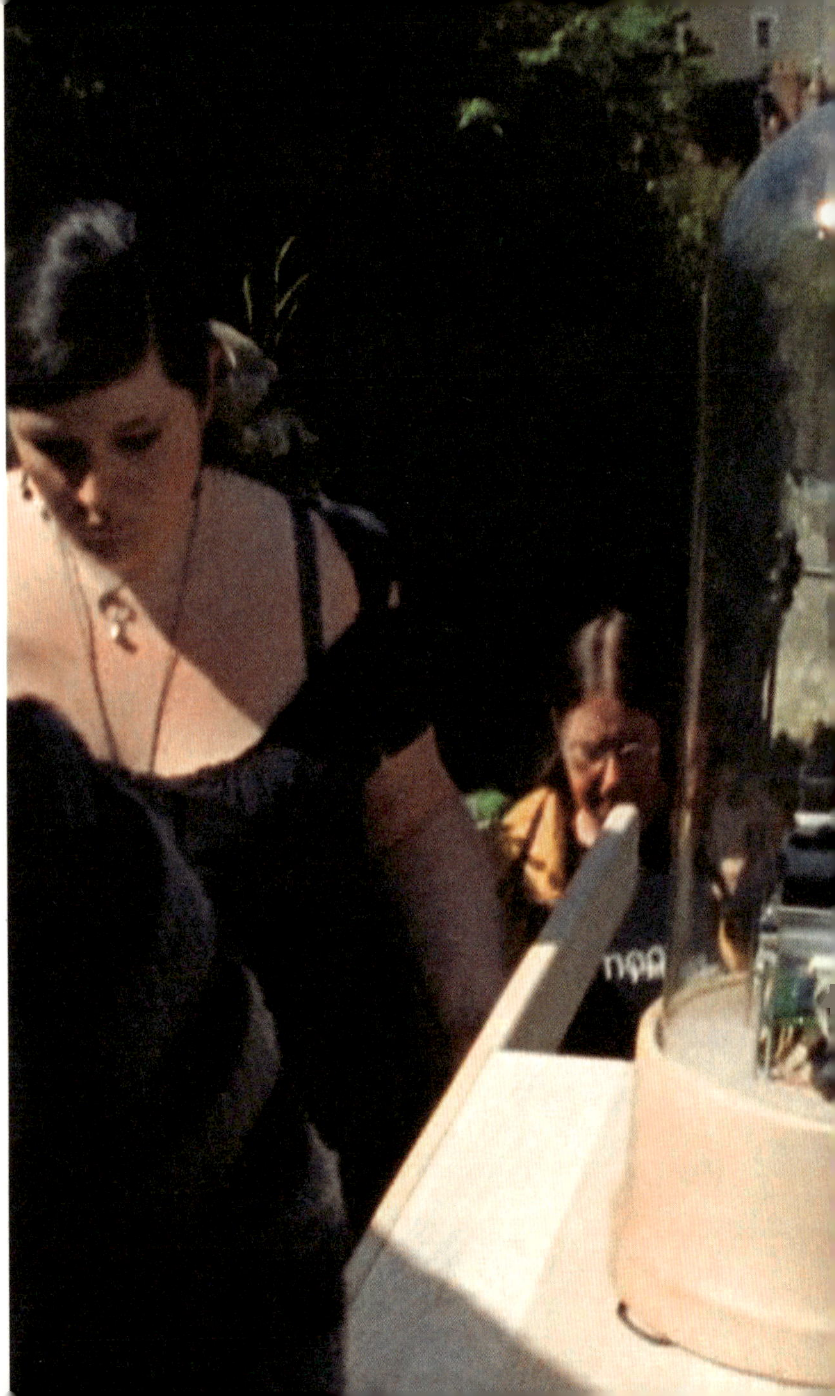

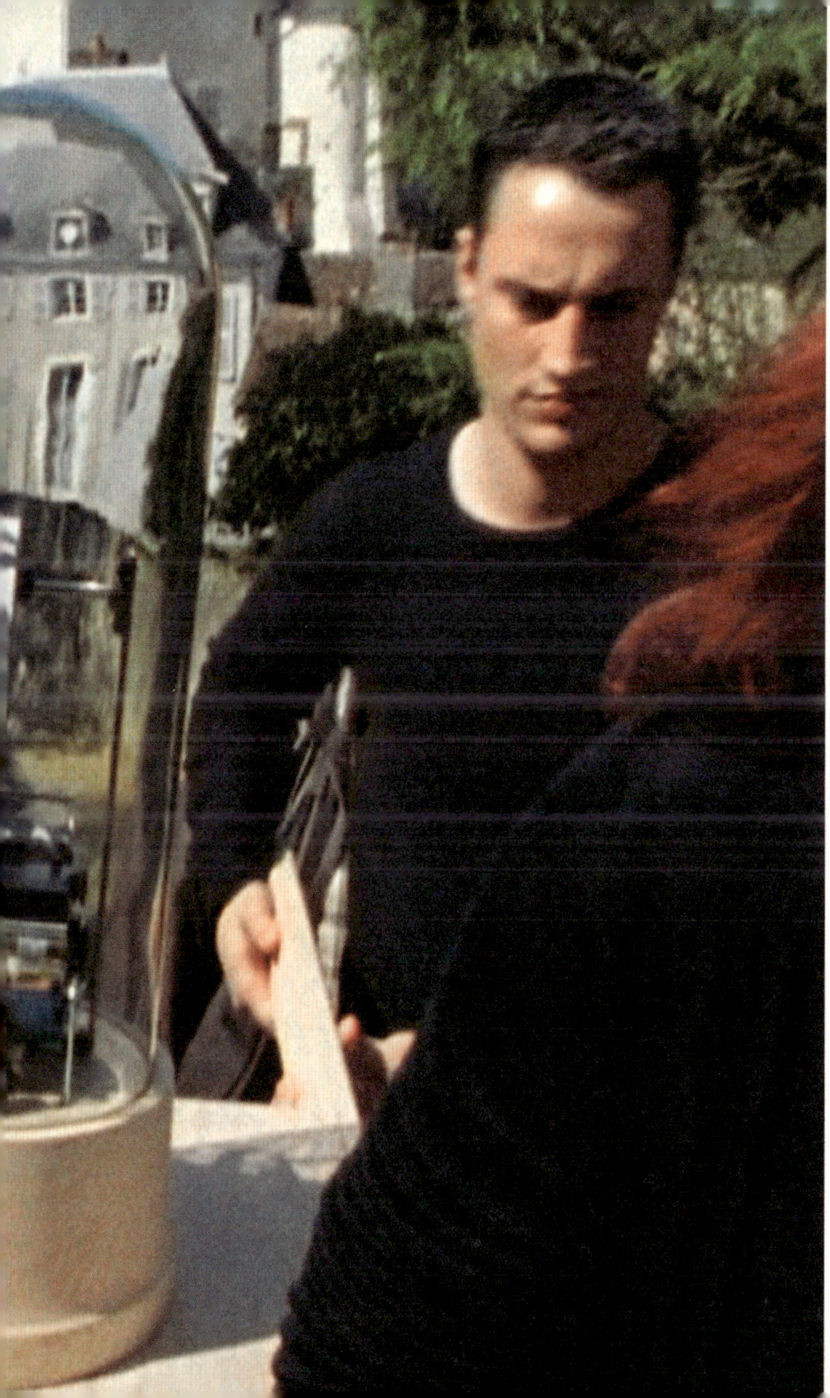

On Excess, Acceleration and Accumulation / L'Excès, l'Accélération et la Dépense, 2012
16 page newspaper in French and English
265mm x 410mm, b/w
First edition of 2000 published by Ikon Gallery
ISBN 978 1 904864 76 9
Distributed in Le Blanc and in Birmingham at the solo exhibition
How To Use Fool's Gold, Ikon Gallery 15th February – 22nd April 2012
(Adapted single-language version reproduced here)

L'EXCÈS,
ON EXCESS,
L'ACCÉLÉRATION
ACCELERATION
ET LA DÉPENSE
AND EXPENDITURE

This newspaper is being produced to coincide with the conclusion of the film project *Second Burial at Le Blanc* by Sarah Browne marking the final end of circulation of the French franc, ten years after the first introduction of the euro, in the village of Le Blanc. The first part of this film was shot in spring 2011 with the participation of local shopkeepers and residents and followed a staged procession of a bespoke ticker-tape count-down clock through the town. This glass-domed mechanism both tracks euro currency exchange rates via wireless internet and works as a countdown clock, printing the days, hours, minutes and seconds until 17th February 2012, when French francs will finally pass from use in the village and nationwide. This clock was carried from the modern Hôtel de Ville in the main square to Château Naillac, the medieval castle that overlooks the village on the far side of the river and houses a small museum. The conclusion of the film will document the events that unfold at the end of the countdown, reflecting on the following questions:

> Ten years after the franc passed from usual use, should this second burial be met with acceptance, joy or grief?
>
> In the midst of the ongoing crisis in the Eurozone, is there really hope for continued life after the death of the national currency—in this case, the franc?
>
> Should we rather be preparing ourselves for a relapse, and to imagine instead life after the death of the euro (staging a *séance* with the franc instead of a funeral?)

Although a real place, the representation of Le Blanc on film enters a realm of fiction, or at least uncertainty. To the Anglophone ear *Le Blanc* sounds like a blank, a void space of disappearance and white noise. It's poetic in the way a place becomes when it's abstracted, distanced from itself. For the purposes of the film, it is considered as a parallel reality or a different time zone, where it is possible to un-tether the imagination and to consider differently a crisis that is happening in parallel, in real time, in the Eurozone.

As a non-expert, this is a crisis of finance that feels fundamentally difficult to find orientation within, let alone to understand in any reliably thorough or methodical way. A problem of both epic and unknowable scale, it is also paradoxically presented in the media as somehow solvable by economic interventions: seemingly rational and scientific methods. However, the kind of wildly divergent speculations being produced by economists, about what would happen should the euro collapse for example, would indicate that economics is not a science at all—not if science is understood as a field of knowledge free of dogma. Scientists would be capable of extrapolating general laws from observation and therefore predicting to some degree of accuracy something about what will happen next.[1]

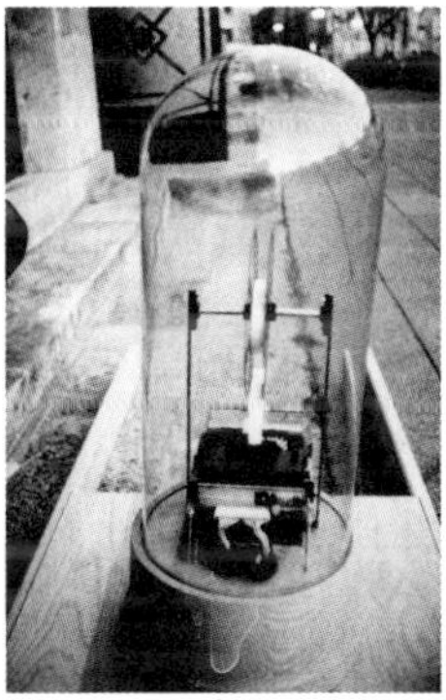

Ticker tape countdown clock at Le Blanc, April 2011. Photo by Lukas Demgenski.

In 1976, Jean Baudrillard wrote in his book *Symbolic Exchange and Death* that the entire financial system is falling into indeterminacy, attributing this dissolution to the loss of the relationship between time and value manifested by financial capitalism. Some years earlier, President Richard Nixon had played his part in this change, cancelling the gold standard and the Bretton Woods system, unfixing the relationship of the US dollar from other currencies and from any material referent of intrinsic value. Where gold circulates because it has value, paper has value because it circulates.

What do you store in a bank? You store time. But is the money that is stored in the bank my past Time, the time that I have spent in the past? Or does this money give me the possibility of buying a future? This is precisely the necessary enigma or secret within the age of financial capitalism, but is it a secret *or an* enigma*? We can say that the secret is something that is hidden in a box. If you find the right key, the secret will become truth. On the other hand, an enigma has no key and no truth... financial capitalism is constructed as an enigma: you cannot find the truth because it is based upon the fact that the truth has dissolved. It is no longer there.*[2]

This conception of time (modern, capitalist) is structured in relation to progress, as a process of growth or even perfectibility. This is a cultural concept as much as an economic criterion, and therefore also has cultural and social effects, particularly an effect of acceleration: growth in productivity for example, demands acceleration in work time. Inflation can also be experienced as a kind of acceleration: the experience of needing more and more time, money, and attention to buy fewer and fewer things, services and experiences. Our brains function in time, and need time in order to give attention and understanding. But attention cannot be infinitely accelerated. It's a limited resource, like many others.[3]

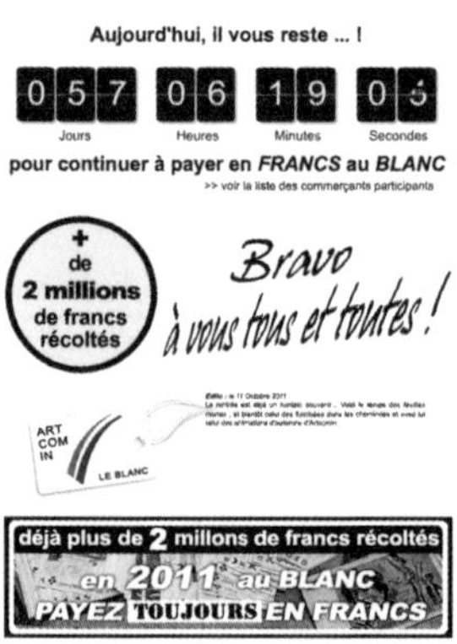

Screen grab from Art' Com' In website, December 2011

Political scientist Susan George and anthropologist Fabrizio Sabelli identify this particular idea of constant economic and developmental growth as the promised hereafter of institutions such as the World Bank that we are encouraged to rush towards. Where 'development' in its biological sense refers to an organism's attainment of its inherent potential, inexorably followed by decay and death, in the Bank's vocabulary this meaning is replaced by a concept of never-ending growth, an everlasting extension into the future where the possibility of a final death is taboo.

This eternal reward can be gained through attending to rigid, quasi-religious practice. Aspects of this discipline include repenting for debts; suffering threats of inflation and misery for sins committed; accepting austerity measures as penance; worshipping the dogmas of growth and competition. George and Sabelli tackle the World Bank in particular as an institution that is as much a political and cultural enterprise as an economic one, assuming a multiplicity of functions, becoming a modern version of what the pioneer sociologist Marcel Mauss called the 'total social phenomenon' (*le fait social total*). Their questions about the Bank are applicable also in a general way to institutions such as the International Monetary Fund (IMF) and the European Central Bank (ECB). These institutions are not powerful because they are purely economic entities, nor are they powerful because they possess some of the characteristics one would expect of an international public service organisation. Their obvious, financial and economic appearance is only the beginning:

Why do we think we need the Bank? For the same reasons we think we need the Church. Frail, imperfect humanity needs constraints, guardrails, continual instruction in, and interpretation of, the doctrine. Those who have not yet reached the full expression of market capitalism and consequent development, those who fall by the wayside, must be goaded along the path to salvation.[4]

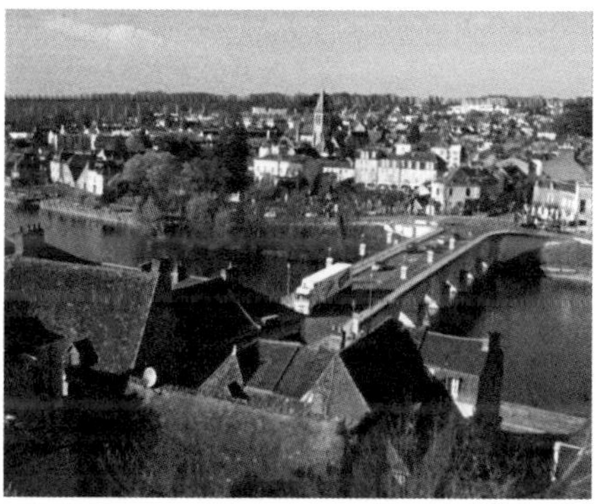

(This and following two pages) Film still from *Second Burial at Le Blanc*, (Sarah Browne, 2011), 16mm colour film, 8'18"

George and Sabelli also highlight an even more basic feature common to the Church and Bank: the belief that they have not only the right but the duty to intervene. Both have 'missions' in the broadest sense; in the Church's case to the heathen; in that of the Bank to the 'less developed' countries.[5] Institutions such as the World Bank, the IMF and the ECB manage to conflate religious and financial understandings of time that valorise the future, convey a sense of deferred promise, justify the existence of present suffering and deny the inevitability of a final, absolute end. The myth of endless growth promises a kind of eternity in the here-and-now, denying entropy and denying the inevitability of death. However since the Club of Rome published the book *The Limits to Growth* in 1972, we have understood that Earth's natural resources are limited—and that social production and expenditure must be redefined according to this knowledge.

This redefinition is difficult to accept, more difficult still to respond to in ways that have the correct balance of urgent pragmatism and urgent imagination. Franco Beradi accuses economists of preferring reality to harmonise with their own supposed laws rather than adjusting their conceptual framework when those laws seem incorrect.[6] Modern culture has equated economic expansion with the future, so that for economists, it tends to be impossible to consider the future independently of economic growth. The direst outcome of such a refusal to adjust a conceptual framework for thinking about the economy or the future would be the failure to recognise changes in the social paradigm.

In November 2011, Irish journalist Fintan O'Toole reflected on a particular week in the Eurozone as an important episode within the ongoing crisis, demonstrating just such a paradigm shift. The article was significant in two respects: first, it pointed out that historical moments aren't sudden changes, but rather points at which something that has been long in the making finally emerges, when something murky crystallises into clarity. Secondly, it discussed the decoupling of capitalism and democracy as evidenced by two events that week in the EU. The first of these was the refusal of 'permission' from Europe for the Greek government to hold a citizen's referendum on the proposed European bailout, and the second was the forced payment by the Irish government to unsecured bank bondholders, under threat from the European Central Bank. O'Toole describes a resultant shift from our received wisdom from the Enlightenment onwards, that democracy and capitalism are at the very least compatible with each other—since the things that were needed in order for capitalism to develop were also conditions for political democracy, such as the breaking of aristocratic power, the free movement of labour, functioning parliaments, taxation to fund mass education and infrastructure and so on.[7]

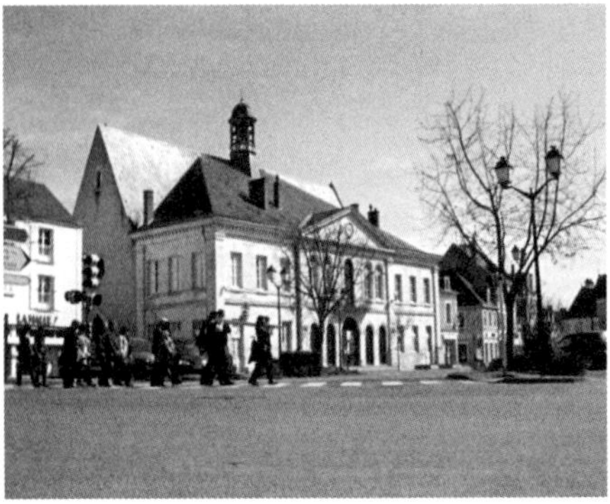

What became dramatically clear [last week] was that this compatibility has ended. The leading form of capitalism – the finance capitalism that has expanded so monstrously over the last thirty years – is no longer compatible with democracy in Europe. And by democracy in this context I mean just the limited, basic form: universal suffrage and sovereign governments. Europe, and the rest of the western world, is thus at a parting of the ways. We can have the form of rapacious finance capitalism that has become the dominant force in our economies and societies. Or we can have democracy. But we can't have both.[8]

At what point during a supposed growth cycle does a financial crisis arise? At what point does a currency rush towards the brink of collapse? By what mystical, mathematical formula can we divine that the end is nigh and intervention is needed – from the ECB for example, or its sister the IMF? In mid November 2011 as Greece appeared to be nearing some such tipping point, it seemed that this 'contagion' within the Eurozone (a striking bodily metaphor of illness or possession) might spread to Italy.[9] This would have been a serious escalation due to the relative size of the Italian economy, the pressure this would exert on the current European bailout facility, and therefore the entire viability of the common currency. By what equation could this precise tipping point be identified? During this week, the particular figure of a 7% key borrowing rate was identified as a threshold of some kind that had been crossed by Greece, Ireland and Portugal, forcing these nations to seek bailouts.[10] George and Sabelli, when querying the World Bank's definition of 'development' and intervention, ask a similar question about orientating ourselves on a curve: if we accept the equation according to which development equals growth equals eternal life, how do we know when we've 'arrived'? The Bank answers this question with arithmetical precision: a country 'graduates' from the status of Bank borrower when its average per capita income reaches \$4.465 in 1991 dollars.[11] In both examples, the attempted isolation of one statistic, one tiny *bit* of information to explain the complexity of the entire situation seems an abstraction that is almost esoteric in its arbitrariness.

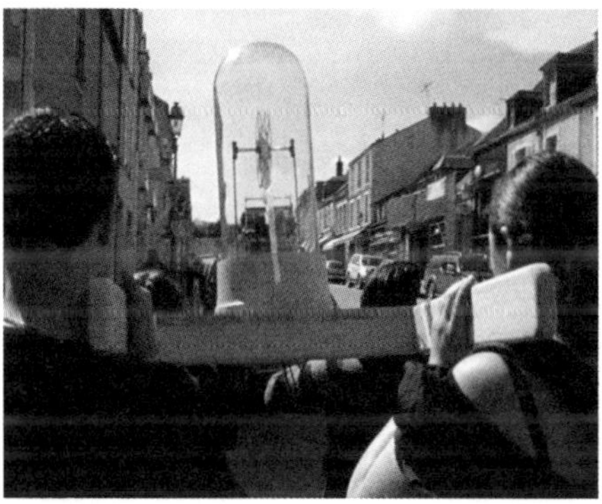

If the world market is the Bank's fundamental organizing principle, price is its instrument. One of the Bank's major articles of faith is 'getting the prices right', which it translates in French as la verité des prix, *the truth of prices. A price has a metaphysical quality because it is supposed to be the invisible point at the intersection between hundreds, thousands, millions of individual transactions. Price, if governments do not meddle by providing subsidies and otherwise distort the natural balance of things, will regulate human activity and necessarily bring order out of apparent chaos.*[12]

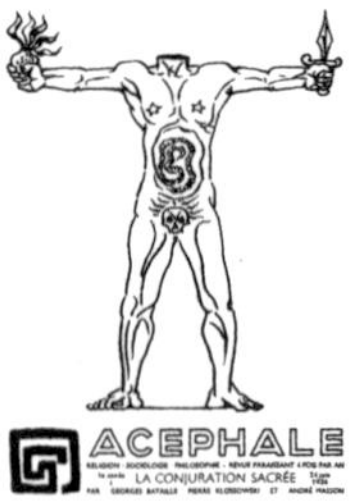

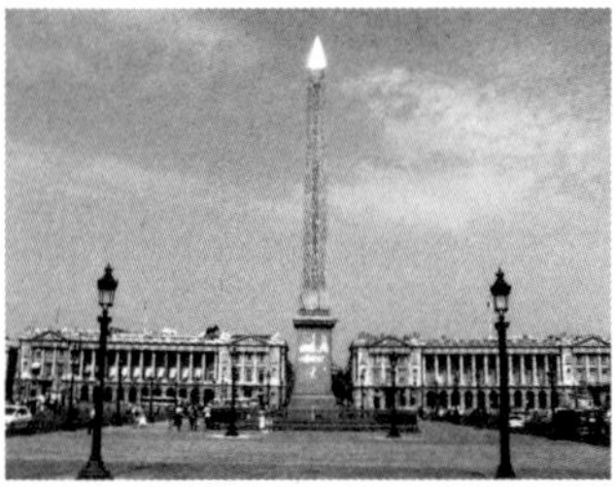

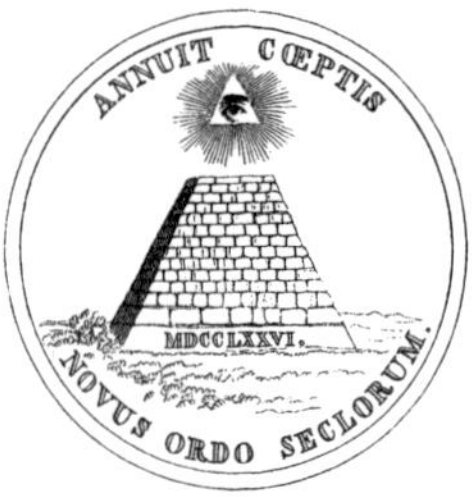

(left) *Acéphale* drawing by André Masson. Emblem of the secret society founded by Bataille and published in the journal of the same name.

(centre) Luxor obelisk, Place de la Concorde, Paris. One of a pair of 3300 year old Egyptian obelisks, both of which were originally located at the entrance to Luxor Temple, Egypt and moved to Paris in 1833. The gold-leafed pyramid cap was added to replace the original missing pyramidion in 1998. 'There was some difficulty in finding an appropriate symbol for the Place de la Concorde, where the images of royalty and the Revolution had proven powerless. But it was contrary to the majesty of the site to leave an empty space, and agreement was reached on a monolith brought back from Egypt. Seldom has a gesture of this type been more successful; the apparently meaningless image imposed its calm grandeur and its pacifying power on a location that always threatened to recall the worst... neither God nor time remained.' — Georges Bataille, 'The Obelisk,' 1936-39.

(right) The Great Seal of the United States (reverse). In 1934, Henry A. Wallace, then the Secretary of Agriculture in President Franklin D. Roosevelt's cabinet, noticed and especially liked the motto *Novus Ordo Seclorum* ('New Order of the Ages') on the Seal, likening it to Roosevelt's New Deal. He suggested to Roosevelt that a coin be made which included the reverse, but Roosevelt instead decided to put it on the one dollar bill.

Finance is wealth without territory, unfixed from place. Where then should we go to talk about finance? Whom should we speak with? It is not easy to identify financial capitalists as individual persons, just as finance is not the monetary counterpart of a certain number of physical goods. There are only mathematical implications, seemingly automatic social outcomes that seem unavoidable. How so to address this faceless, placeless enigma of finance? In their study of the World Bank, George and Sabelli speak of beliefs, faith, doctrine, prophecy, and fundamentalism; of ancestors, initiation, *esprit de corps*, intellectual leadership and rule. Like anthropologist Michael Taussig, in addition to facts and the documentary evidence, they make a few unorthodox sorties they call 'Interludes' into the world of the imagination, pointing out that if the Bank were just a bank, they would have had no reason to call on fiction. Philosopher George Bataille (whose early education included both a Catholic seminary and numismatic studies) is an instructive example too. Active during the rise of Fascism in Europe, his numerous efforts at deeper understanding of and resistance to such a complex social shift involved the adoption of different strategies in parallel—from direct political action and intellectual debate, to a secret society in the forests outside Paris that concerned itself with esoteric ritual and even human sacrifice.[13] Bataille was concerned with developing an idea of 'general economy', a theory that rejected any conventional logic of scarcity and instead focused on a problematic of abundance and excess. (This was tackled however by considering a range of human and social expenditures typically considered outside of economic reach, such as religion, sexuality and death). These ventures (or withdrawals) into storytelling, the arcane and the anthropological, represent a range of alternative ways to grapple with immediate socioeconomic problems that we believe should be comprehensible and solvable in a logical and rational manner. However it's completely possible that this is not true, that such a radical departure into fiction, the imagination or the irrational is exactly what is needed. Where else does finance dwell?

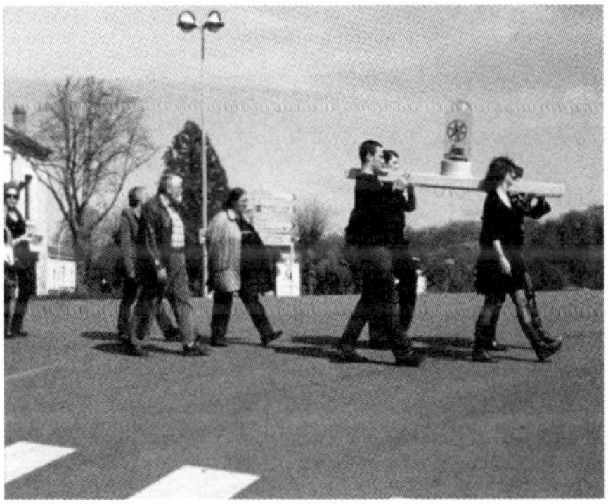

Film still from *Second Burial at Le Blanc*, (Sarah Browne, 2011), 16mm colour film, 8'18"

The clock made for Le Blanc and represented in the film attempts to materialise in a modest way some of these difficult and mobile questions. An amalgamation of digital and analogue technologies, the clock is a device that concentrates the forces of time/price and progress/entropy. It excretes long ribbons of paper information, producing voluminous excess as it counts down to the end, to nothing. Somehow the information it receives from the air and neatly outputs onto paper does not lead to more easily decoded knowledge. Therefore the clock is a peculiar and superstitious kind of object, a deliberate fetish.[14] It asks the question - what will we do when the end comes? It's a device designed to expire, waiting for an ending, just as the word 'finance' is derived from the French verb *to end* - though the kind of ending that's a resettlement of a debt, even retribution.[15] This attitude doesn't presume a catastrophe, nor is it an attempt to will such significance into being where it likely just doesn't exist. There are enough disaster prophecies already, from last year's Christian Rapture—which may or may not have arrived—to next year's end of the Mayan calendar at the winter solstice.[16] Bugarach in the Aude region of France is a tiny village that's home to a 'mystic mountain', said to have inspired both Jules Verne's *Journey to the Centre of the Earth* and Steven Spielberg's *Close Encounters of the Third Kind*.[17] Apparently these are sound enough reasons to make people believe the mountain promises an alien salvation, and the village is suffering already a deluge of visitors seeking shelter from the 2012 Armageddon to come. So there are no shortage of Doomsday prophecies, and no lack of arbitrary dates to attach them to. This film project in Le Blanc is simply an attempt to pin a series of simple questions about a complex issue to one particular time, in one particular place.

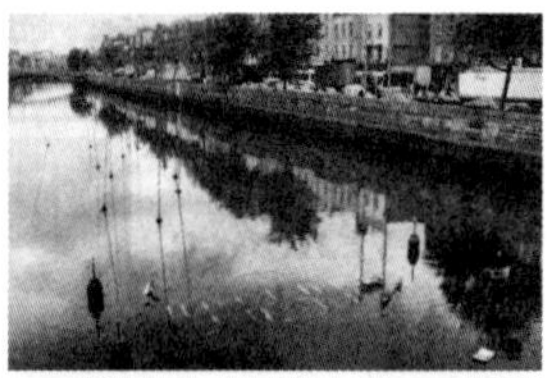

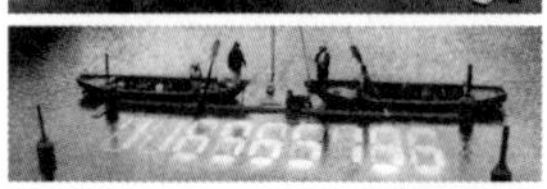

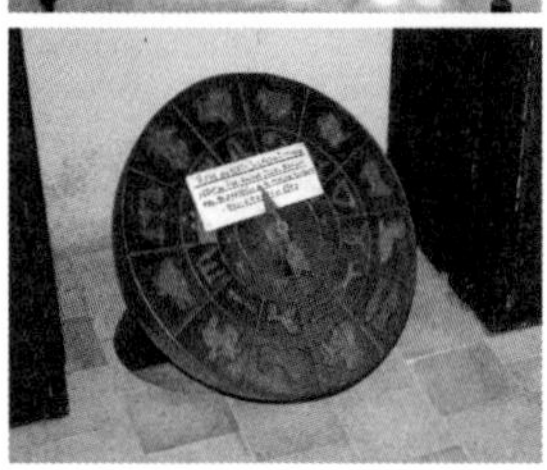

(above and middle) Millenium Countdown Clock, Dublin. Commissioned by the National Lottery, the Millennium Countdown Clock appeared in the river Liffey in March 1996. 10,000 people attended the unveiling, which was televised live. The 12m long timepiece with a digital readout was designed to float just below water level, whether at high or low tide, but by the end of that summer, complaints were made that the digits could not be read, as debris and dirt clogged the green digital display. It was removed in and not placed back in the water. Of the 119 million seconds intended for the clock to countdown, it only ticked away approximately 14 million seconds, leaving about three and a half years of uncounted seconds. http://www.mejewelanddarlin.com/abuseofmonuments.htm Accessed November 10th 2011.

(below) Zodiac clock in Musée des Amis du Blanc, gifted to the town in 1951

Beradi suggests the necessity of disentangling the future (the perception of the future, the concept of the future, and the very production of the future) from the traps of growth and investment as the only way out of the vicious subjugation of life, wealth, and pleasure to finance and its abstraction. The Zapatistas in Mexico, emerging from the jungle in Chiapas in 1994 in an uprising against NAFTA and the privatisation of communal lands, make a similar rallying call for a new understanding of revolutionary time, issuing communiqués that utilise the symbolism of the *caracol* (the snail) and the ear of corn. This will be a slow revolution connected to an indigenous Mayan sense of time—but a slow revolution that is communicated and disseminated by high-speed wireless internet and cellular phone. Beradi's suggestion for us to imagine the future differently lies in the creation of a new form of wisdom—harmonising with the exhaustion that comes with total, or almost total, expenditure:

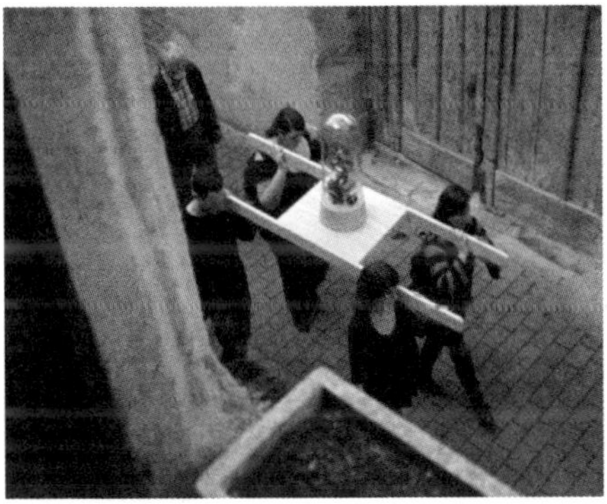

Film still from *Second Burial at Le Blanc*, (Sarah Browne, 2011), 16mm colour film, 8'18"

Exhaustion is a cursed word in the frame of modern culture, which is based on the cult of energy and the cult of male aggressiveness. But energy is fading in the postmodern world for many reasons that are easy to detect. Demographic trends reveal that, as life expectancy increases and birth rate decreases, mankind as a whole is growing old. This process of general aging produces a sense of exhaustion, and what was once considered a blessing—increased life expectancy—may become a misfortune if the myth of energy is not restrained and replaced with a myth of solidarity and compassion. Energy is fading also because basic physical resources such as oil are doomed to extinction or dramatic depletion. And energy is fading because competition is stupid in the age of the general intellect. The general intellect is not based on juvenile impulse, on fighting, winning, and appropriation. It is based on cooperation and sharing.

And so back to Le Blanc, a small and maybe sleepy village in France, for the completion of a film that relates to a currency crisis, an accelerating financial crisis, of much further reaching scale: a place circulating a defunct currency, with a significant population of older and retired people, a 'new town' on one side of the river, and an 'old town' on the other. Where were you when Kennedy was shot, or on September 11th 2001 when the twin towers were destroyed? (On the tsunami on St. Stephen's Day in Asia I was in a treehouse on a Thai island, cutting my toenails, before I had to run away from the wave. On 9/11 I was walking past an electrical store in Dublin and paid little attention to the CNN news feed on the televisions in the window, only later discovering one of my family had been killed.) Momentous events often don't seem all that important when they happen. Disasters, tragedies and triumphs can happen quietly in daily life, acquiring significance and meaning sometimes only in their retelling.

It's unlikely that you will be asked in the future, *where were you at the end of the French franc*? Perhaps you will not even notice its passing, but we will be waiting in Le Blanc.

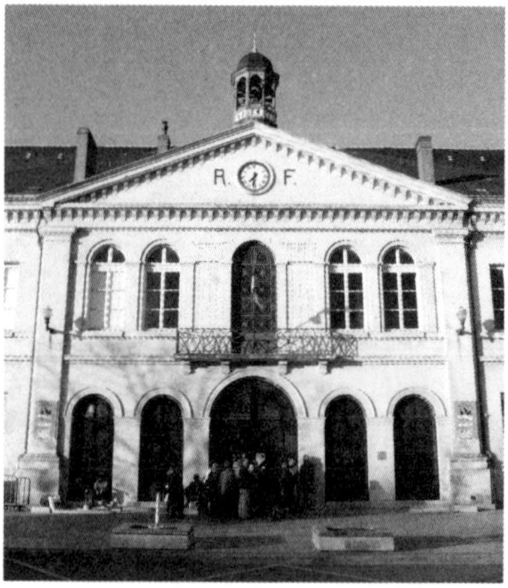

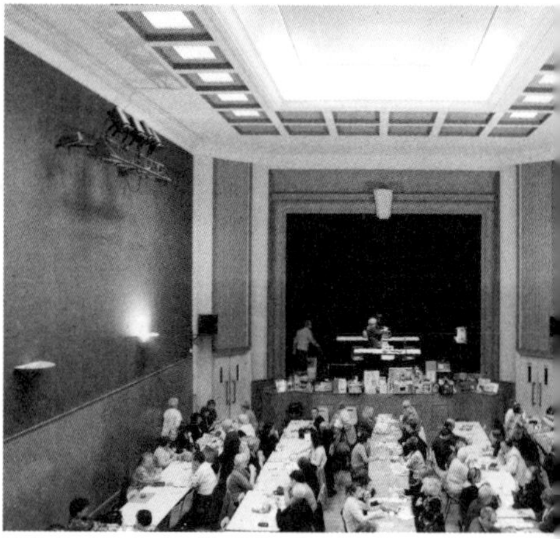

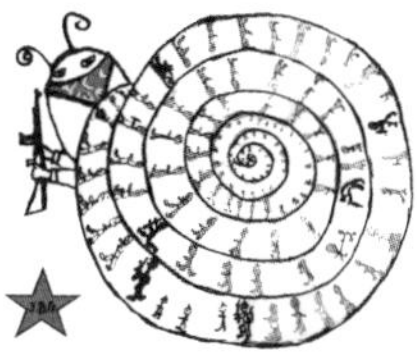

Madre de los Caracole del Mar de Nuestros Sueños (Mother of the Snail of Our Dreams), Junta de Buen Gobierno, Chiapas, Mexico. Subcommandante Marcos explains, how the *caracoles* are clusters of villages, but described as spirals they reach out to encompass the whole world and begin from within the heart. 'The *caracoles* will be like doors to enter into the communities and for the communities to come out; like windows to see us inside and also for us to see outside; like loudspeakers in order to send far and wide our word and also to hear the words from the one who is far away.'

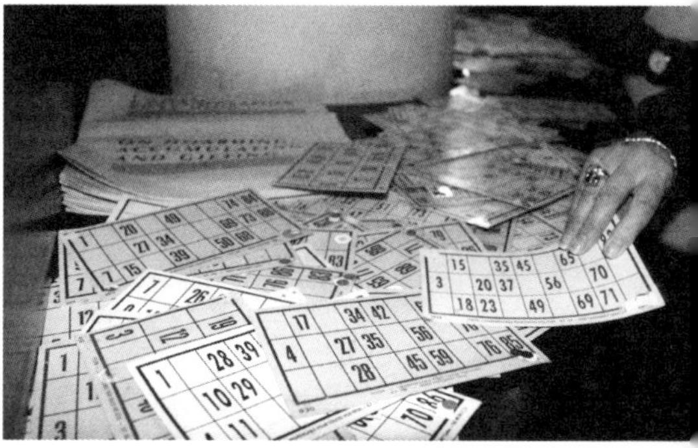

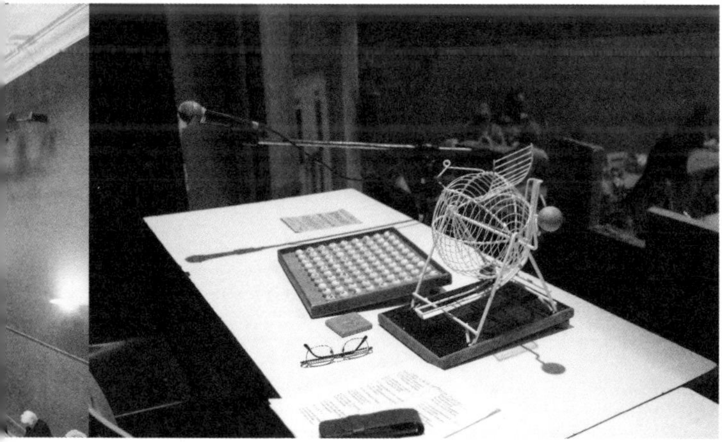

Bingo at the Hôtel de Ville, Le Blanc, April 2011

1 Franco Berardi (Bifo), 'The Future After the End of the Economy,' *e-flux journal #30*, December 2011.
2 Franco Berardi (Bifo), 'Time, Acceleration, and Violence,' *e-flux journal #27*, September 2011.
3 Beradi, ibid.
4 Susan George & Fabrizio Sabelli, *Faith and Credit: The World Bank's Secular Empire*, New York, 1994, p.249.
5 http://www.tni.org/archives/archives_george_parallel Accessed December 16 2011.
6 Franco Berardi (Bifo), 'The Future After the End of the Economy,' *e-flux journal #30*, December 2011.
7 O'Toole qualifies this generalisation, noting that there have been huge tensions in the relationship between capitalism and democracy; that there have been periods when the holders of capital preferred authoritarian or fascist regimes; and that the large-scale inequalities inherent in most forms of capitalism have tended to limit the practice of democracy. The point is simply that the two forces were generally compatible. Fintan O'Toole, 'Triumph of the spivs as democracy is sidelined,' *The* 8 O'Toole, ibid.
9 Headlines include 'German minister admits to euro zone "contagion"' and 'It's not a matter of Eurozone contagion spreading, it's how sick we will get'; http://www.irishtimes.com/newspaper/world/2011/1130/1224308336646.html http://seekingalpha.com/article/313949-it-s-not-a-matter-of-eu-contagion-spreading-it-s-how-sick-we-will-get Both accessed December 16 2011.
10 Pan Pylas, 'Market fears over Italy, Greece ease further,' The Boston Globe, November 11, 2011.
11 http://www.tni.org/archives/archives_george_parallel. Accessed December 16 2011.
12 George & Sabelli, ibid.
13 The groups referred to are *Contre Attaque* (1935-36), the *Collège de Sociologie* (1937-39) and Acephale (1936-39).
14 In the 1600s, 'fetish' was the word derived from the Portuguese *feitiço* (charm, sorcery), from the Latin *facticius* (made by art) from *facere* (to make). *Facticius* in Spanish has become *hechizo* (magic, witchcraft, sorcery). Probably introduced by Portuguese sailors and traders as a

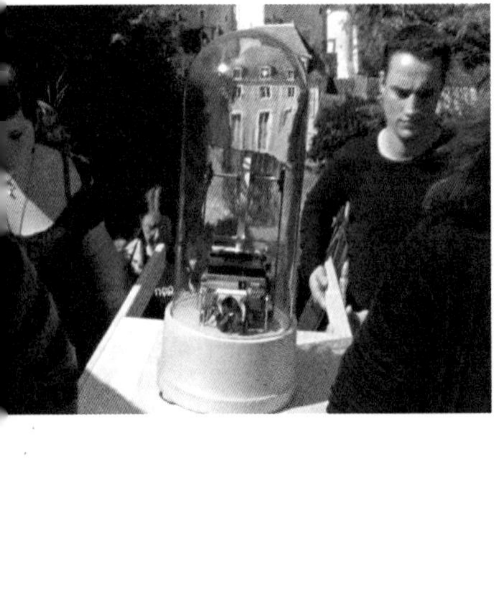

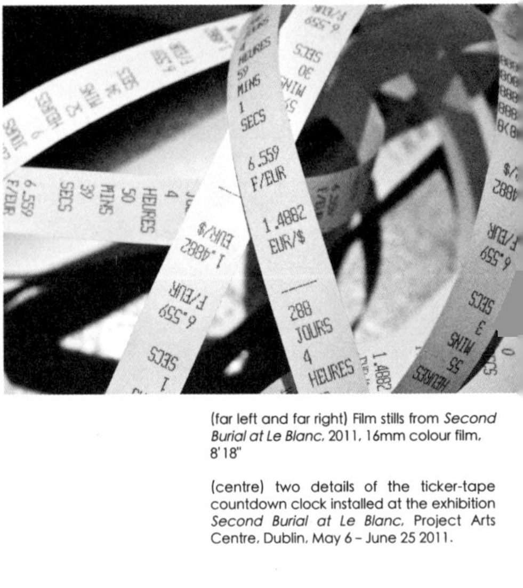

(far left and far right) Film stills from *Second Burial at Le Blanc*, 2011, 16mm colour film, 8'18"

(centre) two details of the ticker-tape countdown clock installed at the exhibition *Second Burial at Le Blanc*, Project Arts Centre, Dublin, May 6 – June 25 2011.

name for charms and talismans worshipped by the inhabitants of the Guinea coast of Africa, it was popularised in anthropology by C. de Brosses' *Le Culte des Dieux Fétiches* (1760), which influenced the word's spelling in English. The figurative sense of somethingirrationally revered' is noted in American English from 1837, and the purely psychosexual understanding of the fetish was not recorded until the very late 1800s in the writings of Henry Havelock Ellis.

15 As an activity, the verb 'to finance' has its origins in the late fifteenth century, when it meant'to ransom.' The sense of managing money is not recorded until the early 1800s, and that of furnishing a venture with money is recorded still later in that century. As a noun, the word is known from around 1400, when it meant 'an end, settlement, retribution,' from the French noun *fin*. The notion is of 'ending' (by satisfying) something that is due (cf. Gk. *telos* 'end' ; pl. *tele* 'services due, dues exacted by the state, financial means.' From the mid fifteenth century, the French senses gradually were brought into English also.

16 Any individual or religious group that has dogmatically predicted the day of the Rapture, a practice referred to as 'date setting', has been thoroughly embarrassed and discredited, as the predicted date of fulfillment has invariably come and gone without event. Some of these individuals and groups have offered excuses and 'corrected' target dates, while others have simply released a reinterpretation of the meaning of the scripture to fit their current predicament, and then explained that although the prediction appeared to have not come true, in reality it had been completely accurate and fulfilled, albeit in a different way than many had expected. The most recent prediction was for October 21st 2011.

17 http://www.telegraph.co.uk/news/newstopics/howaboutthat/ufo/8217251/Bugarach-the-mystery-surrounding-the-village.html. Accessed December 16 2011.

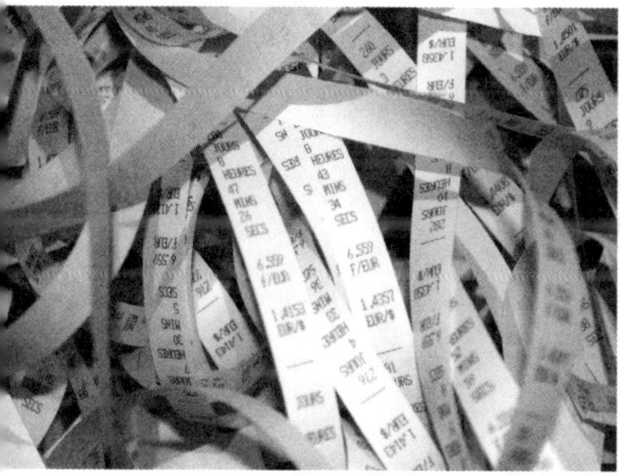

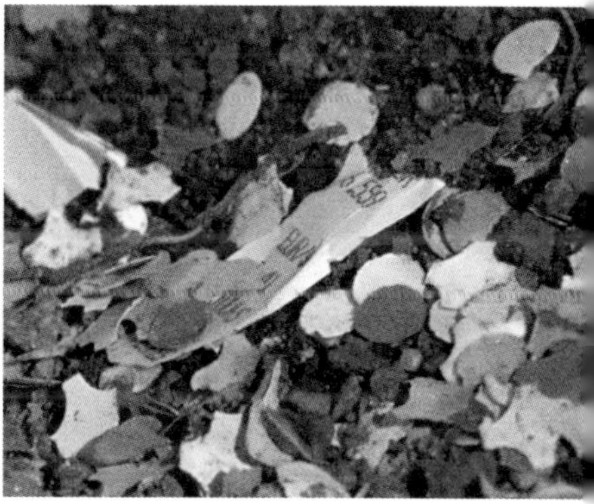

Le Dernier franc / Le Blanc, 2011
Correction fluid on map of France
1040mm x 940mm

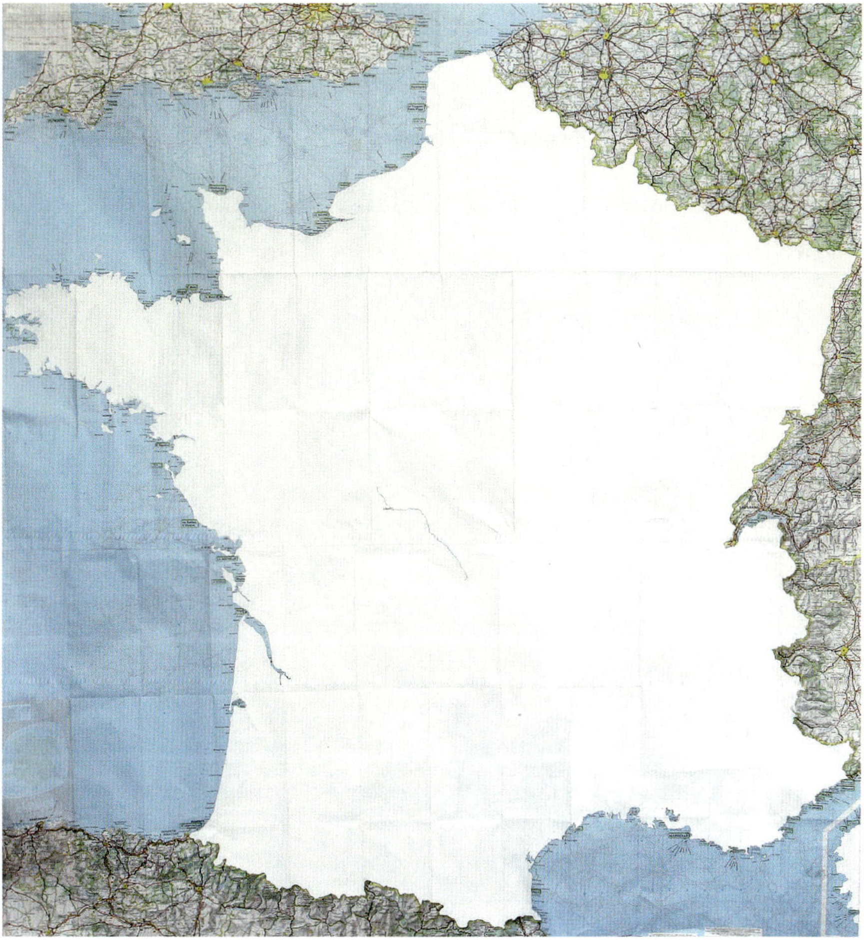

Le Blanc / Le Dernier franc, 2011
Watercolour pencil and ink on French franc banknote
77mm x 120mm

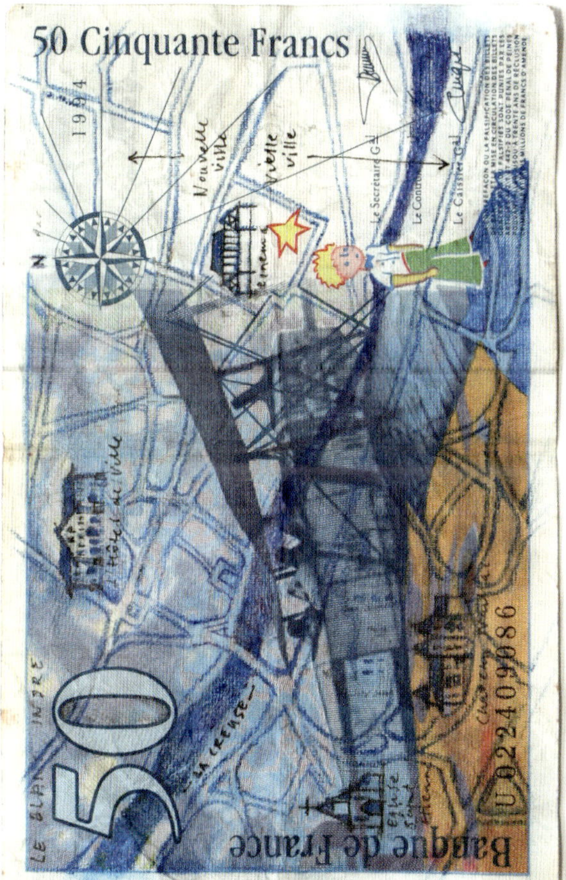
50 Cinquante Francs
1994
N
Nouvelle ville
vieille ville
Le Secrétaire Gal
Le Caissier Gal
Hôtel de Ville
LA CREUSE
LE BLANC INDRE
50
Banque de France
U 022409086

Alternative Currencies

Chris Lee

> **The reversal of modern capitalism involves not only the struggle against material bondage and invisible forms of repression, but also, from the outset, the creation of many alternative set-ups.**
>
> —Felix Guattari [1]

DISTRESS RELIEF PROGRAM
Slow circulation of money is the principal cause of the faltering economy. Money as a medium of exchange increasingly vanishes out of working people's hands. It seeps away into channels where interest flows and accumulates in the hands of a few, who do not return it back to the market for the purchasing of goods and services but withhold it for speculation. As money is an indispensable wheel in the machine of production, an accumulation of great sums in a few hands means a gigantic danger for peaceful production. Every time the flow of money is interrupted, so is the exchange of goods and services, with a consequent fall in employment. Uncertainty about the state of the economy makes the owner of money careful, causing him/her to hoard it or to spend it reluctantly. He or she distrusts investment. Money circulation is thus slowed down, the turnover of goods and services shrinks and jobs disappear. Such a situation denies incentives to the population, threatening peace and wealth with destruction. Whole nations and states are under the threat of ruin. Our small place cannot liberate the world, but we want at least to give a sign. In the Wörgl area the sluggish, slow-circulating National Bank currency shall be replaced with a medium of exchange with a better circulating performance than ordinary money. 'Certified Compensation Bills' shall be issued in denominations of 1, 5 and 10 Schillings and put into circulation. The council shall issue the Bills and the public shall undertake to accept such Bills at their full nominal value in payment for goods and services. In order to turn around the economy of the township, public works shall be planned and paid for with the same Bills.

—Michael Unterguggenberger, Mayor of Wörgl's proposal to the Austrian town's welfare committee read at a meeting on July 5th, 1932, in the midst of the Great Depression.[2]

How Banks Create Money

fig. 1

Bank 1 creates money into existence by issuing loans. Only a fraction of this created value is actually backed by what is held by the accounts of commercial banks at the central bank. (a) gets four unites and must repay three units of interes. (b) and (c) get three units each, and pay one and two units interest respectively.

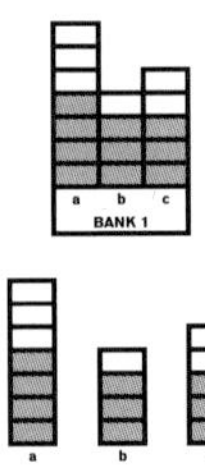

fig. 2

(a) manages to earn three units of profit off of (b) and (c), and pay off it's loan with interest. Now (b) and (c) will not be able to pay off their loans because there is not enough real currency in circulation. Bank 1 has made three units profit.

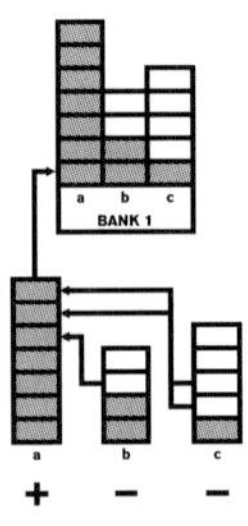

fig. 3

(b) and (c) have to earn their interest payments off of another or from Bank 2's network of debtors. This exacerbates the imbalance among both bank's debtors (debtors (b) and (d) are virtually crushed here), and the network of debt expands when Bank 2 debtors have to earn profit from Bank 3 debtors and so on... Thus an artificial scarcity of money is maintained in spite of the fact that much of the money didn't really exist in the first place.

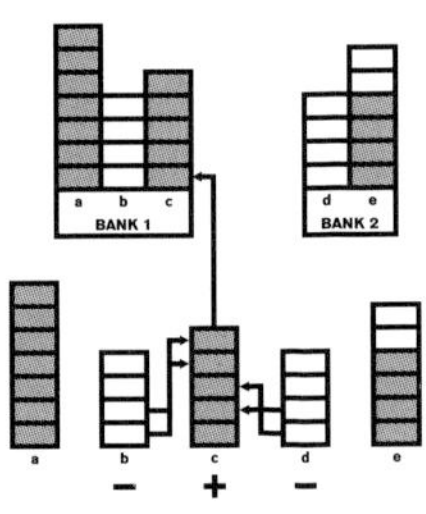

The Wörgl experiment proposed above was for a brief period immensely successful, reviving the economic activity of the town, setting it apart as an oasis amidst the darkest days of the Great Depression. Unfortunately, in the year following its inception, the Wörgl experiment was ended abruptly by the Austrian Supreme Court. News of its 'miraculous' success had spread, with 170 mayors from municipalities across Austria attending a briefing in Vienna willing to adopt Wörgl's economic strategy. This was perceived as a threat by Austria's National Bank, because it violated its exclusive privilege and right to issue currency. In the decades following however, countless adaptations, variations and improvements on mayor Unterguggenberger's experiment have appeared all over the world, with incidences rising particularly in times of economic crisis.

The court decision to terminate this experiment in alternative currency begs the question: Why would a supposedly democratic government deny a community of its citizens the possibility and ability to improve its economic circumstances, especially in light of the clear success of Wörgl? Who was it that sought to deny the will of 170 mayors, and what exactly were they trying to protect?

Initiated under the conditions imposed by a hegemonic exchange standard (fiat currencies), counter-hegemonic ones (alternative currencies) can be read as a rejection of centralised dominance, and as assertions towards the actualisation of economic democracy.[3] They figure a space of conflict inhabited by subjects constructed and constituted by their respective network standards (e.g. Wörgl's 'Certified Compensation Bills' vs. Austrian Schillings). Richard Day, author of *Gramsci is Dead: Anarchist Currents in the Newest Social Movements*, may classify the alternative currency movement as a form of one of these non-hegemonic 'newest social movements.'

These networked subject positions can be understood via the concept of 'network power' whose central notion, the *standard* (i.e. the English language, or the US dollar), the thing that facilitates social coordination and cooperation, generates 'gravitational force.' To sketch this idea out briefly by way of example, let's examine the network power of the English language.

The more people there are that use this linguistic standard, the more attractive it becomes to prospective students of language over say, Iroquoian. This would be for the very simple fact that learning English would grant one access to a broader network of people with whom one may cooperate or socialise. What you have here is a freely made choice to learn English, granted, perhaps often as a backdrop to a coercive situation. But even without the explicit coercion, the choice in its substance *resembles* a coerced one, particularly because the number of acceptable alternatives for ways of being and ways of cooperating become more limited, as smaller languages die out. This is not to claim that one should necessarily resist network power on the basis that its effects resemble coercion; but a cause for resistance would appear when a desire to disconnect from the network is frustrated by the lack of viable alternatives, effectively creating conditions of 'imprisonment.'[4]

This is the kind of situation we are in when we assume that there is only one legitimate form of money that precludes the possibility of alternatives. The moment this becomes troubling is when we realise money is not a neutral medium that is the inevitable outcome of rationalised exchange systems: rather, it's a medium whose indubitably coercive bias is a carry-over from a time when overt expressions of power were more commonplace. For example, gold's ascension as a universal standard was fraught with violent conflict because it was a political medium to the extent that possession afforded one status and the capacity to exert power. The danger with it was that it could also be stolen (along with its attendant status and power).[5] What characterised this condition, and what proponents of alternative currencies often argue is that a fundamental flaw of contemporary money—from the perspective of a desire for a just and egalitarian society—is that scarcity inevitably leads to coercion. A brief examination of the ancient origins of our current money system gives further insight.

Anthropologist (and anarchist) David Graeber, in an article for the journal *Mute*, traces a genetic link between debt, slavery and money. Through outlining a brief history of debt, he argues that its contemporary form (money) carries a coercive code, programmed into this most common exchange medium thousands of years ago that culminates in the effect of divorcing value from the labourer. Graeber begins by drawing a basic connection between slavery and debt. He posits that the coerced condition of slavery is one where all other debts (obligations) that were owed previous to one becoming a slave are negated, and all that remains is the ostensibly absolute debt to one's owner. The reason for this is that a defining feature of slavery is that slaves can be bought and sold on a market, ultimately making the debt quantifiable. He maintains that there are two consequences.

The first was that debt made it possible to formulate our modern understanding of money, and that it produced as a result the '...market: an arena where anything [could] be bought or sold, because all objects are (like slaves) disembodied from their former social relations and exist only in relation to money.'[6] The second consequence is a little more elaborate. Essentially it goes that sovereign rulers, wanting to maintain their position in the social hierarchy, encouraged markets for a handful of reasons. One was that they were highly convenient, because rather than levy directly from the subject population whatever they needed (say, weapons for soldiers to conquer more territory for the extraction or capture of more gold), the presence of markets of available goods and services meant that they could acquire those things with relatively more convenience. The other reason was that these purchases could be made on the terms dictated by the ruler, namely through gold and silver (which were naturally scarce), that only they had control over, by being able to mobilise the resources to extract it directly through mining and indirectly through conquest. They would essentially 'dump' this currency on the population, then by way of coercive legitimacy demand it back in the form of taxes. This would thereby institute a form of structural domination fixing the orientation of production to the needs of the army, which was paid with the same coin.

The difficulty with this picture however, is that this process is not self-evident. Gold and silver must have emerged as universal standards among a more general population prior to this event in order for the sovereign's coercive power to be directed towards the acquisition and distribution of these rare metals. The moment of 'dumping' is in effect a moment of the imposition of an institution: thus the relational logic of the taxed subject whose debt is to the state corresponds here to the debt logic of slavery.

The logics of slavery and scarcity can be transposed to the operations of banks, which create money (backed by the legitimacy of the state) into existence (out of thin air) in the form of loans.[7] These banks also charge interest on top of the principal sum, which the borrower must pay back as well. The trouble begins when we find that all the other money in circulation, a pool from which the borrower must extract enough to pay back the principal *and* interest, is also created out of thin air as loans. So the actual amount of money in circulation is always smaller than the amount of money that is legally owed to the banks. This represents a condition of artificial scarcity, and also means that in order for some people to pay off their loans, others must default. The infinite availability of money would negate its value. The system functions in spite of its continuous production of defaulters. In fact it could be said that the system maintains its kinesis because its continuous production of defaulters give substance to the threat of poverty—a disciplinary mechanism driving economic productivity.[8]

It would be a mistake however, to dismissively characterise money as 'inhumane' on the basis of its origins and coercive structural effects. Instead, what is needed is a clearer differentiation between the functionality of *money* from that of *currency*.

In Douglas Rushkoff's recent book *Life, Inc.*, such a distinction is outlined. Rushkoff elaborates that money derives its value from the scarcity of commodities (whether it is naturally scarce like gold, or artificially scarce like fiat currencies, i.e. dollars, euros, yen, etc. whose actual differences are cosmetic), and is therefore biased toward storage and accumulation. As such, commodities (and commodity money)[9] as a form of storage for scarce value are more effective for conducting trade over greater distances of space and time. *Currency*, on the other hand, is biased toward spending and circulation. Its 'currents' facilitate function, and sustain life. Currency acts as a token of flow, a 'map' if you will, of exchange, a marker of social relations, and the medium of an economy that is only as scarce as the people living and working within that economy. An ideal situation would have the amount of currency in circulation corresponding directly to the amount of value produced and put into the economy—no more, no less.[10]

The question remains how alternative currencies are brought into and kept in circulation. Usually, and particularly in an alternative currency's early stages, there is a strong reliance on the so-called 'network of trust.'[11] Invariably, these projects require large commitments of time to develop this initial trust built through 'leg work,' which often involves educating local businesses about the potential benefits of involvement. Some alternative currency projects evolved from casual small bartering clubs, while others have emerged as a direct response to crisis. The network of barter clubs of Argentina's *Red Global de Clubes de Trueque Multirecíproco*, (Global Network of Multi-Reciprocal Exchange Clubs, in response to the Argentine economic crisis of the late 90s to early 00s) is an example that developed from both conditions. Originating as a project of three ecologists who began holding barter club markets in their front yards, it saw at its peak relatively widespread participation with localised clubs across the country (about 7% of the population). Clubs began to falter when the worsening condition of the formal economy drove increasing numbers of people to join these barter clubs. The system experienced shock from counterfeiting and hyperinflation due to a growing percentage of spending currency into the system without necessarily contributing production to it. In addition, between 2002 and 2003 unemployment insurance was made available by the state to 2.5 million people (coincidentally, about 7% of the population), thereby increasing the volume of the official peso in circulation among those in the barter club networks.[12] Although in this instance, participation was relatively wide-spread and robust, the ease with which it faltered suggests that it was for many, more of a self-organised temporary relief measure, than a substantially committed political project.

The long term cohesion of an alternative currency system could however have very much to do with the ability to relate the use of these alternatives to a larger project or desire that often transcends the conventional value metrics of our current money system. The Liberty dollar from the United States for example, attracted users by aligning itself with right-libertarian values such as minimising state intervention and a return to a currency system backed by silver and gold. On US Independence Day in 2007, Liberty Dollars issued commemorative coins that featured Republican congressman Ron Paul, who advocates the gradual dissolution of the Federal Reserve.[13]

The actual graphic design of some currencies can also provide insight in the way that they construct subject networks based on common values or desires. For example, local symbols, personalities and landscapes are often depicted on alternative coin and paper currencies. They affirm a local or regional identity as in the illustrated landscapes of the currency issued by the secessionist Cascadia Bioregion.[14] The depiction of John the Baptist on the Florin, as opposed to the Earthly emperor Frederick II, suggests an economic network constituted by religious affiliation;[15] or the depiction of the Statue of Liberty on Liberty dollars makes an appeal to the original ideals of the American constitution, implicitly protesting its usurpation by the Federal Reserve and Treasury Department.[16] However, in an echoing of the fate of the Wörgl currency, the Liberty Dollar attracted hostile attention from the state and has been shut down.[17] What we might deduct from these stories is that underlying all currency initiatives (whether explicitly stated or not) is their capacity to contest the network power of hegemonic standards, and a desire for economic democracy.

By perceiving economic networks as discreet subject positions, we can begin to articulate a politics of networks, instead of continuing with the unexamined assumption that networks and standards are neutral, objective, and inevitable phenomena outside of the possibility of contestation. Counter-hegemonic alternative currencies manifest as a form of direct-action, characterised by an agonistic conflict of standards. While in Chantal Mouffe's concept of agonistic democracy, subject positions vie for hegemony, in this '*economic* agonistic democracy,' the alternatives do not necessarily attempt to annihilate the hegemonic standard, but challenge the hegemonic bias and performatively pluralise the space of exchange standards and sources of legitimacy. Ultimately, alternative currencies represent a collective insistence on economic self-determination. It certainly remains to be seen if the recent proliferation of alternative systems could give form to the notion of economic democracy.

1 Félix Guattari, *Autonomia: Post-political Politics*, Semiotext(e), Los Angeles, 2007, p.109.
2 http://www.sunshinecable.com/~eisehan/woergl.htm. Accessed March 14, 2010.
3 To be precise about the term 'democracy', I use it in the sense that is advocated by Chantal Mouffe, and characterised by agonistic forms of conflict where oppositional subject positions vie for hegemony.
4 The concept of network power is thoroughly developed in the book by David Singh Grewal, *Network Power: The Social Dynamics of Globalization*, Yale University Press, New Haven & London, 2008
5 David Graeber. 'Debt: The First Five-Thousand Years' *Mute*, Vol. 2 #12, June 2009, p. 68. Graeber has subsequently expanded this essay into a recently published book of the same name.
6 Graeber. ibid, p. 65.
7 The political legitimacy of the state is derived from its monopoly on violence. The legitimacy of official fiat currencies is thus derived from the state's capacity to carry out taxation through either direct or structural coercion. The state's propensity to use force to acquire through taxation, let's say sea shells, would render sea shells official and legitimate. It is also worth considering that what makes the design of a passport or money 'functions' negatively, in the sense that the presentation of counterfeit, when it is discovered as such is met with disciplinary violence.
8 Poverty meaning the exclusion from a network of value, where value is not initially created *from* labour, but the speculative investment *in* labour through wages.
9 For example: since August 15, 1971, the US dollar could be considered commodity money when President Richard Nixon unilaterally cancelled the convertibility of the US dollar to gold, the so-called *gold standard*.
10 It should go without saying that alternative currencies do not necessarily preclude the need for voluntarism and charity for those who cannot for whatever reason work, or parallel 'gift' economies, for example. It is not my opinion that the monetisation of all aspects of social life are desirable even with alternative currency systems.
11 While 'network of trust' seems to be the commonly used phrase in discussions about alternative currencies, it might be (before the network approaches a certain degree of complexity) more appropriate to model such a system in a way that can express the metrics of a 'hierarchy of trust,' rather than a diffused polyvalent network of nodes, ie. Elaine has made more satisfactory transactions with Jerry than with George. Thus, George is more likely to be marginalised until the network is substantial enough that his trust metrics find a level of equivalence among a sub-network. Conversely, extreme trust hierarchy imbalances might present as contradictory to the ideals of empowerment with alternative currencies. Through the positive feedback loop of trust, those who possess more can continue to increase their acquisition of it, while those with less continue to struggle for recognition.
12 The *Crédito*, which became the standard currency of the exchange network, was pegged to the Argentine peso, which was at that time pegged to the US dollar. http://en.wikipedia.org/wiki/Crédito. Accessed March 17, 2010.

13 Paul decided to enter politics the same day the US dollar became a commodity. He later remarked that after that day, all money would be '*political* money rather than money of real value...' http://en.wikipedia.org/wiki/Ron_paul, accessed March 16, 2010, my emphasis.

14 The Cascadian Bioregion roughly defined encompasses parts of the Alaskan Panhandle, British Columbia, Idaho, Washington, Oregon, northern California and western Montana. 'Bioregions are geographic areas having common characteristics of soil, watershed, climate, native plants and animals... A bioregion refers to both the geographical terrain and a terrain of consciousness—to a place and the ideas that have developed about how to live in that place.' (http://cascadia-bioregion.tripod.com, accessed March 16, 2010) Although Cascadians strive for independent nationhood, they reject the chauvinism of nationalism, and instead advocate 'bioregionalism' as a political form.

15 Originally minted in Florence in the mid-13th century. By the 14th century, a hundred and fifty European states and local authorities issued their own variations.

16 Ron Paul and Liberty dollars claims that the Treasury Department's monopoly on issuing fiat currency is unconstitutional. They argue that the constitution does not authorise the government to create legal tender (money backed by force of law). They also claim that these tokens of exchange are protected under the first amendment, which protects freedom of speech.

17 Its founder was indicted by a federal grand jury with several counts of violating the United States criminal code, including conspiracy, mail fraud, and 'one count of uttering, passing, and attempting to utter and pass, silver coins in resemblance of genuine U.S. coins in denominations of five dollars or greater...'
http://en.wikipedia.org/wiki/Liberty_dollar#Federal_Government_response, accessed March 17, 2010.

Common Knowledge, 2007—ongoing
Flowers pressed between books and mounted on paper with notations in pencil
Each piece 330mm x 250mm
Installation view at *Unto This Last,* Raven Row, London, 2010

March 2008
Wild primroses pressed in *The Wisdom of Crowds* by James Surowiecki, 2004

December 2008
Gareth says Ginko (Venice Giardini) in Ernesto Laclau, *On Populist Reason*, 2005

December 2009
Berlin shrub (Bauhaus Archiv) in R.L. Stevenson's *An Apology For Idlers*, 1877/2009

January 2010
Tulip (gift from Ana in Finland) in *Keeping Rabbits and Poultry on Scraps*, 1941/2008

February 2010
Pansies in *Militant Modernism*, Owen Hatherly, 2009

March 2010
Daffodils (Mam's garden) in Ariel Levy's *Female Chauvinist Pigs*, 2006

April 2010
Forget-me-nots in *Capitalist Realism*, Mark Fisher, 2009

May 2010
Bluebells in Glenn Adamson's *Thinking Through Craft*, 2009

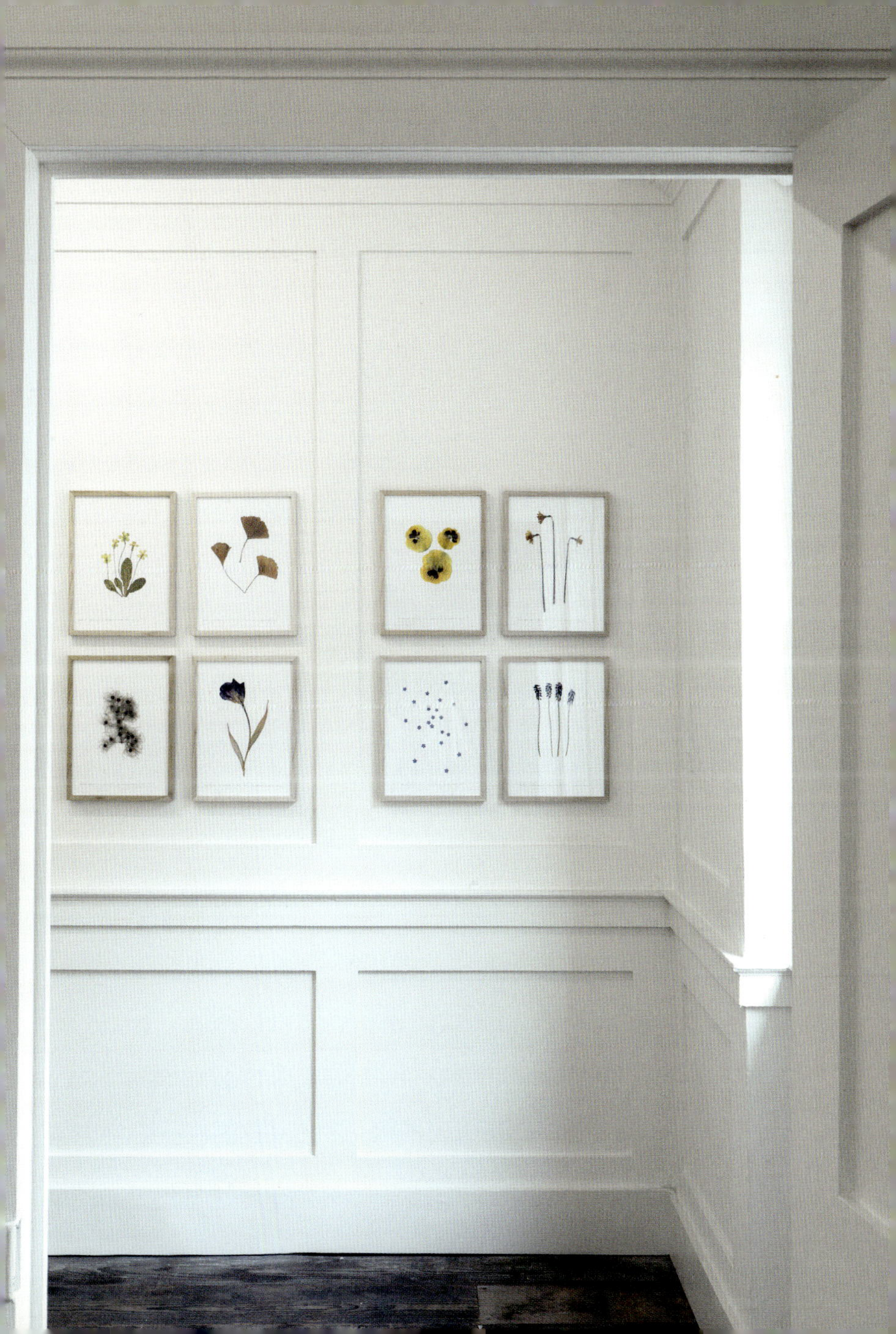

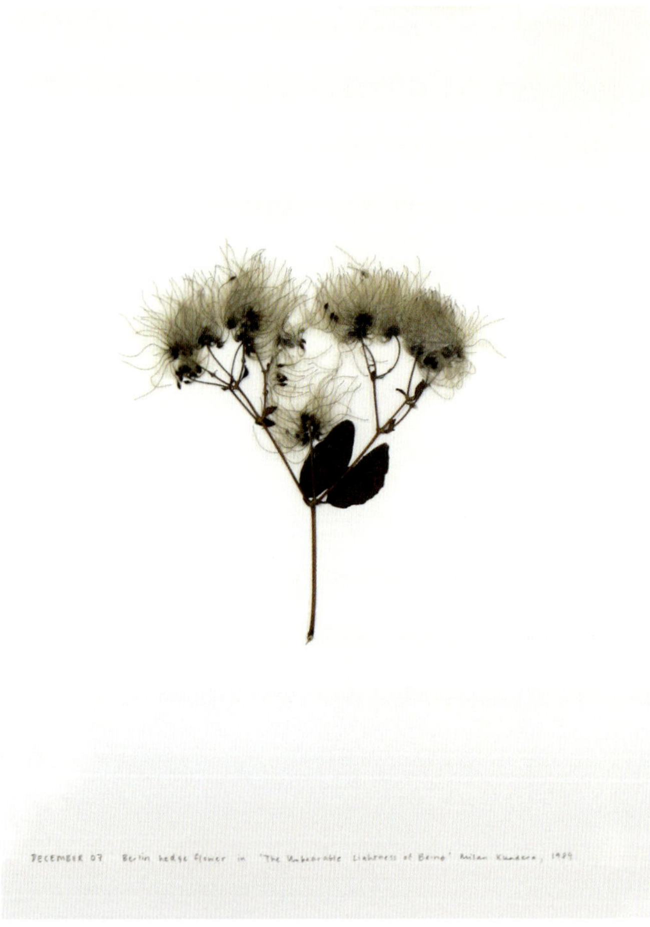
DECEMBER 07 Berlin hedge flower in 'The Unbearable Lightness of Being' Milan Kundera, 1984

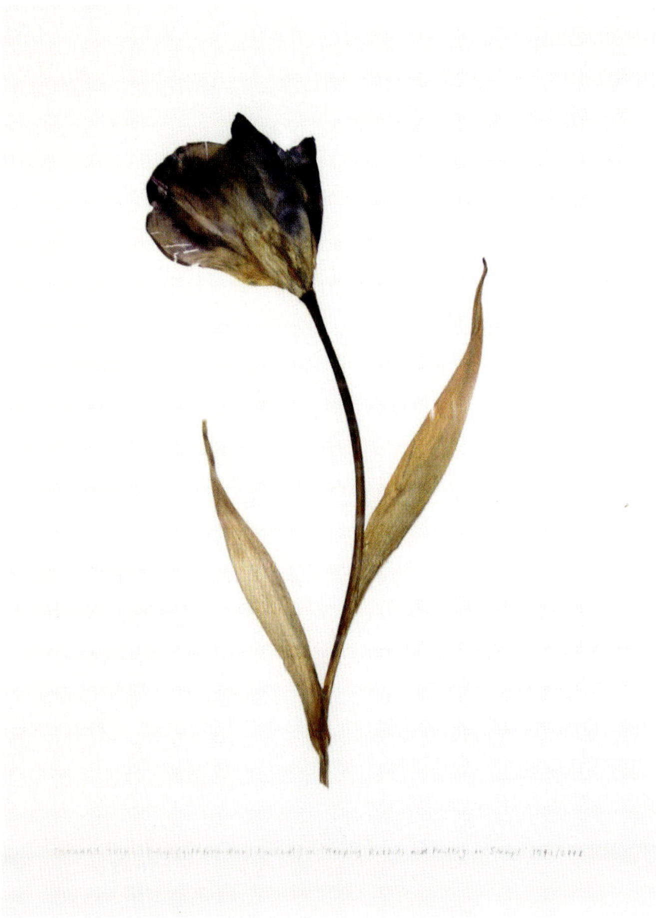

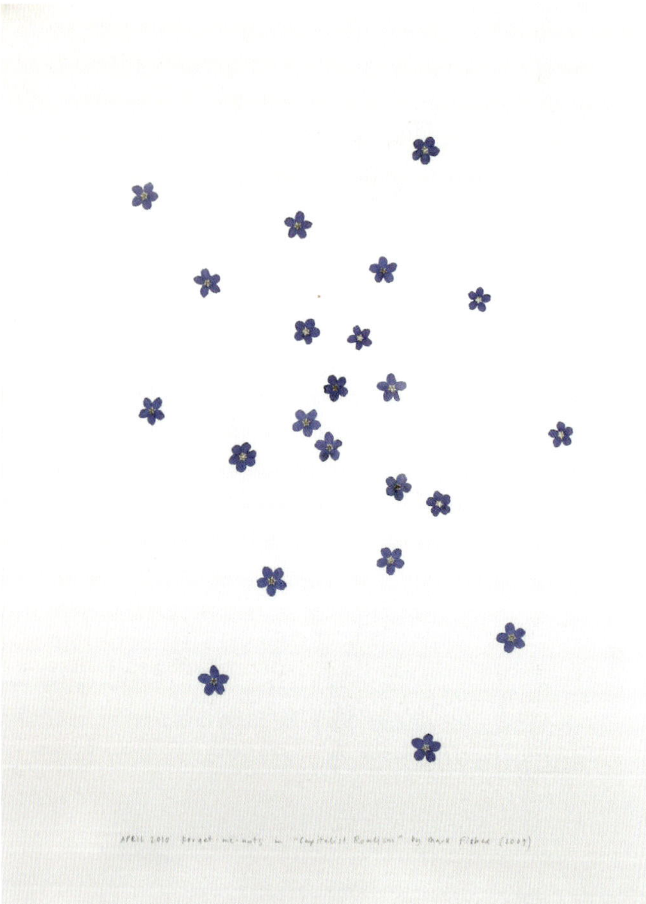
APRIL 2010 forget-me-nots in "Capitalist Realism" by Mark Fisher (2009)

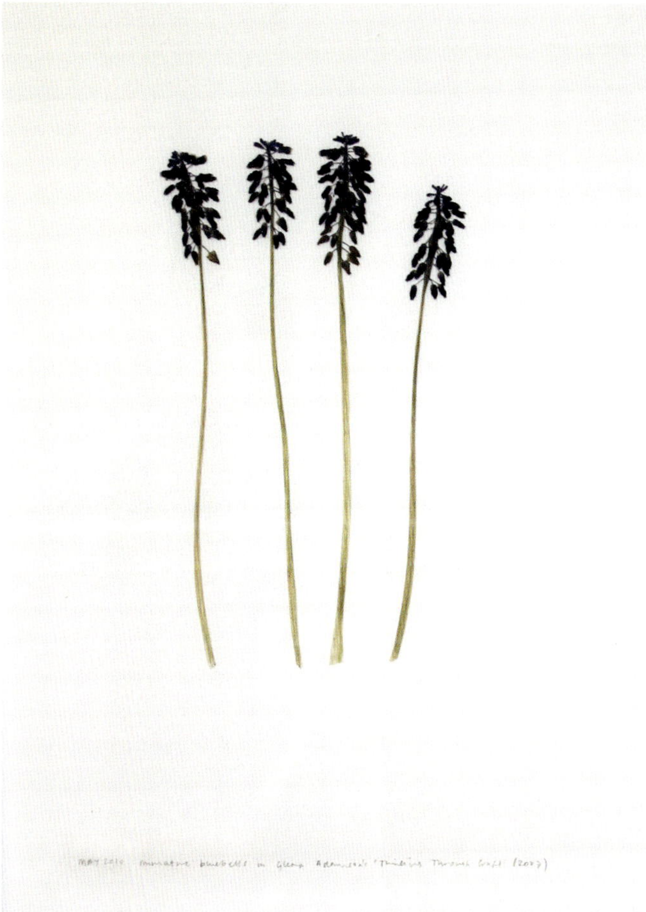
MAY 2010 miniature bluebells in Glenn Adamson's 'Thinking Through Craft' (2007)

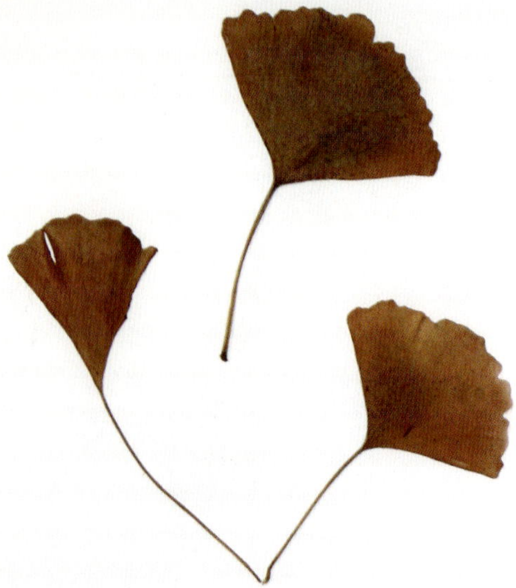

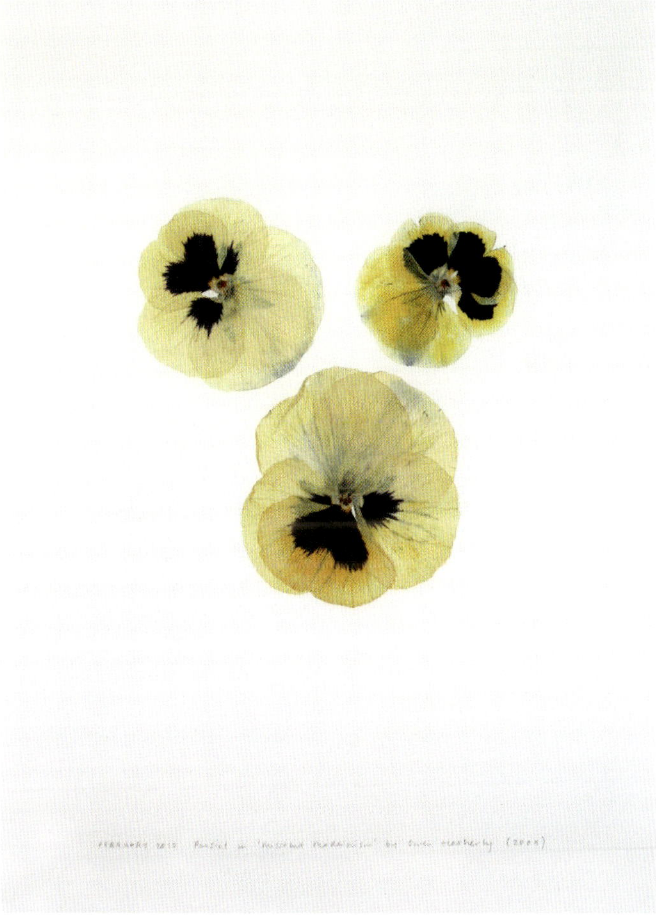

The Original Affluent Society

Marshall Sahlins

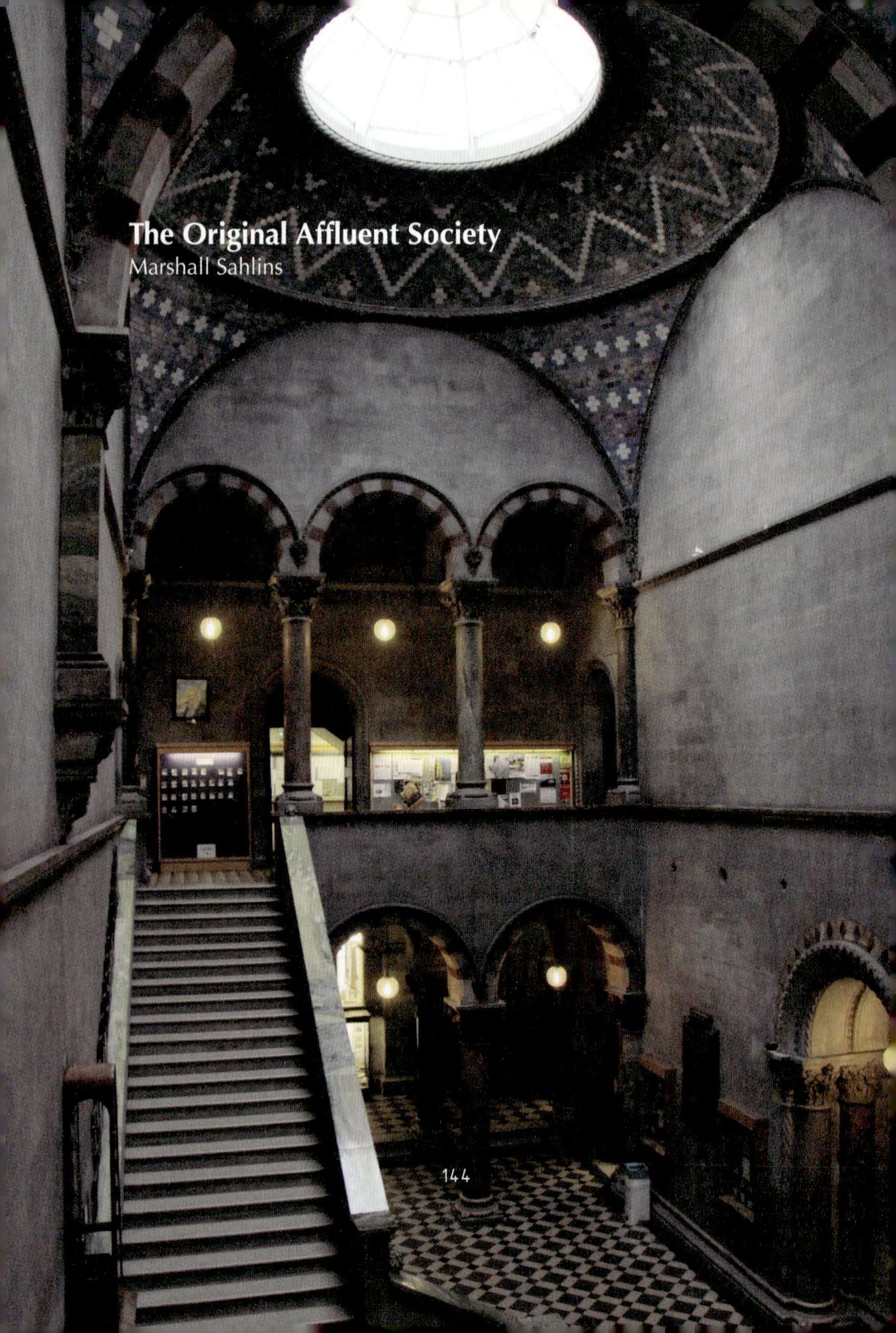

If economics is the dismal science, the study of hunting and gathering economies must be its most advanced branch. Almost universally committed to the idea that life was hard in the Paleolithic, our textbooks compete to convey a sense of impending doom, leaving one to wonder not only how hunters managed to live, but whether, after all, this was living. The spectre of starvation haunts these pages. His technical incompetence is said to enjoin continuous work just to survive, affording him neither respite nor surplus, hence not even the 'leisure' to 'build culture'. Even so, for all his efforts, the hunter pulls the lowest grades in thermodynamics—less energy/capita/year than any other mode of production. And in treatises on economic development he is condemned to play the role of the bad example: the so-called 'subsistence economy.'

The traditional wisdom is always refractory. One is forced to oppose it polemically, to phrase the necessary revisions dialectically: in fact, this was, when you come to examine it, the original affluent society. Paradoxical, that phrasing leads to another useful and unexpected conclusion. By the common understanding, an affluent society is one in which all the people's material wants are easily satisfied. To assert that the hunters are affluent is to deny then that the human condition is an ordained tragedy, with the man the prisoner at hard labour of a perpetual disparity between his unlimited wants and his insufficient means.

'Mere subsistence economy,' 'limited leisure save in exceptional circumstances,' 'incessant quest for food,' 'meagre and relatively unreliable' natural resources, 'absence of an economic surplus,' 'maximum energy for a maximum number of people'—so runs the fair average anthropological opinion of hunting and gathering. But the traditional dismal view of the hunters' fix is also pre-anthropological and extra-anthropological, at once historical and referable to the larger economic context in which anthropology operates. It goes back to the time that Adam Smith was writing, and probably to a time before anyone was writing. Probably it was one of the first distinctly Neolithic prejudices, an ideological appreciation of the hunter's capacity to exploit the earth's resources most congenial to the historic task of depriving him of the same.

That sentence of 'life at hard labour' was passed uniquely upon us. Scarcity is the judgment decreed by our economy—so also the axiom of our Economics: the application of scarce means against alternative ends to derive the most satisfaction possible under the circumstances. And it is precisely from this anxious vantage that we look back upon hunters. But if modern man, with all his technological advantages, still hasn't got the wherewithal, what chance has this naked savage with his puny bow and arrow? Having equipped the hunter with bourgeois impulses and Paleolithic tools, we judge his situation hopeless in advance.[1] Yet scarcity is not an intrinsic property of technical means. It is a relation between means and ends. We should entertain the empirical possibility that hunters are in business for their health, a finite objective, and that bow and arrow are adequate to that end.[2] But still other ideas, these endemic in anthropological theory and ethnographic practice, have conspired to preclude any such understanding.

The anthropological disposition to exaggerate the economic inefficiency of hunters appears, notably by way of invidious comparison with Neolithic economies. Hunters, as Lowie put it blankly, 'must work much harder in order to live than tillers and breeders.'[3] On this point evolutionary anthropology in particular found it congenial, even necessary theoretically, to adopt the usual tone of reproach. Ethnologists and archaeologists had become Neolithic revolutionaries, and in their enthusiasm for the Revolution spared nothing denouncing the Old (Stone Age) Regime. Including some very old scandal. It was not the first time philosophers would relegate the earliest stage of humanity rather to nature than to culture: 'A man who spends his whole life following animals just to kill them to eat, or moving from one berry patch to another, is really living just like an animal himself.'[4] The hunters thus downgraded, anthropology was free to extol the Neolithic Great Leap Forward: a main technological advance that brought about a 'general availability of leisure through release from purely food-getting pursuits.'[5]

There is nothing either to the convention that hunters and gatherers can enjoy little leisure from tasks of sheer survival. By this, the evolutionary inadequacies of the Paleolithic are customarily explained, while for the provision of leisure the Neolithic is roundly congratulated. But the traditional formulas might be truer if reversed: the amount of work (per capita) increases with the evolution of culture, and the amount of leisure decreases. Hunters' subsistence labours are characteristically intermittent, a day on and a day off, and modern hunters at least tend to employ their time off in such activities as daytime sleep. In the tropical habitats occupied by many of these existing hunters, plant collecting is more reliable than hunting itself. Therefore, the women, who do the collecting, work rather more regularly than the men, and provide a greater part of the food supply. Man's work is often done. On the other hand it is likely to be highly erratic, unpredictably required; if men lack leisure, it is then in the Enlightenment sense rather than the literal. When Condorcet attributed the hunter's unprogressive condition to want of 'the leisure in which he can indulge in thought and enrich his understanding with new combinations of ideas,' he also recognised that the economy was a 'necessary cycle of extreme activity and total idleness.'

This 'prosperity' depends as well upon an objectively low standard of living. It is critical that the customary quota of consumables (as well as the number of consumers) be culturally set at a modest point. A few people are pleased to consider a few easily-made things their good fortune: some meagre pieces of clothing and rather fugitive housing in most climates; plus a few ornaments, spare flints and sundry other items such as a few pieces of quartz, all to be carried in skin bags. For most hunters, such affluence without abundance in the nonsubsistence sphere need not be long debated. A more interesting question is why they are content with so few possessions—for it is with them a policy, 'a matter of principle,' and not a misfortune.[6] Want not, lack not. But are hunters so demanding of material goods because they are themselves enslaved by a food quest 'demanding maximum energy from a maximum number of people,' so that no time or effort remains for the provision of other comforts? Some ethnographers testify to the contrary that the food quest is so successful that half the time people seem not to know what to do with themselves. On the other hand, *movement* is a condition of this success, more movement in some cases than others, but always enough to rapidly depreciate the satisfactions of property. Of the hunter it is truly said that wealth is a burden. In his condition of life, goods can become 'greviously oppressive,' as Gusinde observes, and the more so the longer they are carried around. Certain food collectors do have canoes and a few have dog sleds, but most must carry themselves all the comforts they possess, and so only possess what they can carry themselves.

The hunter, one is tempted to say, is 'uneconomic man.' At least as concerns nonsubsistence goods, he is the reverse of that standard caricature immortalised in any *General Principles of Economics*, page one. His wants are scarce and his means (in relation) plentiful. Consequently he is 'comparatively free of material pressures,' has 'no sense of possession,' shows 'an undeveloped sense of property,' is 'completely indifferent to any material pressures,' manifests a 'lack of interest' in developing his technological equipment.

In this relation of hunters to worldly goods there is a neat and important point. From the internal perspective of the economy, it seems wrong to say that wants are 'restricted,' desires 'restrained,' or even that the notion of wealth is 'limited.' Such phrasings imply in advance an Economic Man and a struggle of the hunter against his own worse nature, which is then finally subdued by a cultural vow of poverty. The words imply the renunciation of an acquisitiveness that in reality was never developed, a suppression of desires that were never broached. Economic Man is a bourgeois construction—as Marcel Mauss said, 'not behind us, but before, like the moral man.'

Current low opinions of the hunter-gathering economy need not be laid to Neolithic ethnicentrism, however. Bourgeois ethnocentrism will do as well. The existing business economy, at every turn an ideological trap from which anthropological economics must escape, will promote the same dim conclusions about the hunting life. Is it so paradoxical to contend that hunters have affluent economies, their absolute poverty notwithstanding? Modern capitalist societies, however richly endowed, dedicate themselves to the proposition of scarcity. Inadequacy of economic means is the first principle of the world's wealthiest peoples. The apparent material status of the economy seems to be no clue to its accomplishments; something has to be 'easily satisfied' either by producing much or desiring little. The familiar conception, the Galbraithean way, makes assumptions particularly appropriate to market economies: that man's wants are great, not to say infinite, whereas his means are limited, although improvable: thus, the gap between means and ends can be narrowed by industrial productivity, at least to the point that 'urgent goods' become plentiful.

The market-industrial system institutes scarcity, in a manner completely unparalleled and to a degree nowhere else approximated. Where production and distribution are arranged through the behaviour of prices, and all livelihoods depend on getting and spending, insufficiency of material means becomes the explicit, calculable starting point of all economic activity.[7] The entrepreneur is confronted with alternative investments of finite capital, the worker (hopefully) with alternative choices of renumerative employ, and the consumer... Consumption is a double tragedy: what begins in inadequacy will end in deprivation. Bringing together an international division of labour, the market makes available a dazzling array of products: all these Good Things within a man's reach—but never all within his grasp. Worse, in this game of consumer free choice, every acquisition is simultaneously a deprivation, for every purchase of something is a foregoing of something else, in general only marginally less desirable, and in some particulars more desirable, that could have been had instead.

Hunting and gathering has all the strengths of its weaknesses. Periodic movement and restraint in wealth and population are at once imperatives of the economic practice and creative adaptations, the kinds of necessities of which virtues are made. Precisely in such a framework, affluence becomes possible. Mobility and moderation put hunters' ends within range of their technical means. An undeveloped mode of production is thus rendered highly ineffective. The hunter's life is not as difficult as it looks from the outside. In some ways the economy reflects dire ecology, but it is also a complete inversion. Reports on hunters and gatherers of the ethnological present—specifically those in marginal environments—suggest a mean of three to five hours per adult worker per day in food production. Hunters keep banker's hours, notably less than modern industrial workers (unionised), who would surely settle for a 21-35 hour week.

The conclusion is put conservatively when put negatively: hunters and gatherers need not work longer getting food than do primitive cultivators. Extrapolating from ethnography to prehistory, one may say as much for the Neolithic as John Stuart Mill said of all labour-saving devices, that one was never invented that saved anyone a minute's labour. The Neolithic saw no particular improvement over the Paleolithic in the amount of time required per capita for the production of subsistence; probably, with the advent of agriculture, people had to work harder.

This is the era of hunger unprecedented. Now, in the time of the greatest technical power, starvation is an institution. Reverse another venerable formula: the amount of hunger increases relatively and absolutely with the evolution of culture. This paradox is my whole point. Hunters and gatherers have by force of circumstances an objectively low standard of living. But taken as their *objective*, and given their adequate means of production, all the people's material wants can usually be easily satisfied. The evolution of economy has known, then, two contradictory movements: enriching but at the same time impoverishing, appropriating in relation to nature but expropriating in relation to man. The progressive aspect is, of course, technological. It has been celebrated in many ways: as an increase in productivity, an increase in division of labour, and increased freedom from environmental control. Taken in a certain sense, the last is especially useful for understanding the earliest stages of technical advance. Agriculture not only raised society above the distribution of natural food resources, it allowed Neolithic communities to maintain high degrees of social order where the requirements of human existence were absent from the natural order. Enough food could be harvested in some seasons to sustain the people while no food would grow at all; the consequent stability of social life was critical for its material engagement. Culture went on then from triumph to triumph, in a kind of progressive contravention of the biological law of the minimum, until it proved it could support human life in outer space—where even gravity and oxygen were naturally lacking.

The world's most primitive people have few possessions, *but they are not poor*. Poverty is not a certain small amount of goods, nor is it just a relation between means and ends; above all it is a relation between people. Poverty is a social status. As such it is the invention of civilisation. It has grown with civilisation, at once as an invidious distinction between classes and more importantly as a tributary relation—that can render agrarian peasants more susceptible to natural catastrophes than any winter camp of Alaskan Eskimo. What are the real handicaps of the hunting-gathering *praxis*? Not 'low productivity of labour' if existing examples mean anything. But the economy is seriously afflicted by the imminence of diminishing returns. Beginning in subsistence and spreading from there to every sector, an initial success seems only to develop the probability that further efforts will yield smaller benefits. This describes the typical curve of food-getting within a particular locale. A modest number of people usually sooner than later reduce the food resources within convenient range of camp. Thereafter, they may stay on only by absorbing an increase in real costs or a decline in real returns: rise in costs if the people choose to search further and further afield, decline in returns if they are satisfied to live on the shorter supplies or inferior foods in easier reach. The solution, of course, is to go somewhere else. Thus the first and decisive contingency of hunting-gathering: it requires movement to maintain production on advantageous terms.

But this movement, more or less frequent in different circumstances, more or less distant, merely transposes to other spheres of production the same diminishing returns of which it is born. The manufacture of tools, clothing, utensils, or ornaments, however easily done, becomes senseless when these begin to be more of a burden than a comfort. Utility falls quickly at the margins of portability. The construction of substantial houses likewise becomes absurd if they must soon be abandoned. Hence the hunter's very ascetic conceptions of material welfare: an interest only in minimal equipment, if that; a valuation of smaller things over bigger; a disinterest in acquiring two or more of most goods; and the like. Ecological pressure assumes a rare form of concreteness when it has to be shouldered. If the gross product is trimmed down in comparison with other economies, it is not the hunter's productivity that is at fault, but his mobility.

Still this much history can always be rescued from existing hunters: the 'economic problem' is easily solvable by Paleolithic techniques. But then, it was not until culture neared the height of its material achievements that it erected a shrine to the Unattainable: *Infinite Needs*.

1 It deserves mention that contemporary European-Marxist theory is often in accord with bourgeois economics on the poverty of the primitive. Cf. N. Boukharine, *La Théorie du matérialisme historique*, Editions Athropos, Paris, 1967; Ernest Mandel, *Traite d'economie marxiste*, vol. 1, Julliard, Paris,1962; and the economic history manual used at Lumumba University.

2 Elman Service for a very long time almost alone among ethnologists stood out against the traditional view of the penury of hunters. This text owes great inspiration to his remarks on the leisure of the Arunta as well as to personal conversations with him. *Profiles in Ethnology,* New York, 1963, p.9.

3 Robert H. Lowie, *An Introduction to Cultural Anthropology*, Reinhart, New York, 1946, p.13.

4 Robert J. Braidwood, *Prehistoric Men*, Chicago Natural History Museum Popular Series, Anthropology, Number 37, 1957, p.122.

5 Robert J. Braidwood, *The Near East and the Foundations for Civilisation*, Oregon State System of Higher Education, Eugene, 1952, p.5. Cf. Franz Boas, *Race, Language and Culture*, Free Press, New York, 1940, p.285.

6 Martin Gusinde, *The Yamana*, Human Relations Area Files, Connecticut, 1961, p.2.

7 On the historically particular requisites of such calculation, see Helen Codere, *Fighting with Property*, American Ethnological Society Monograph 18, Augustine, New York, 1968.

The Original Affluent Society *comprises the first chapter of Sahlins' iconic book,* Stone Age Economics, *first published in 1972. This was the same year as think tank The Club of Rome published* The Limits to Growth, *an explicit challenge to classical economics and an understanding of capitalism's possibility for continued growth and expansion. Notably, these two books were prescient of the 1970s oil and gas crises, brought about by the attitudes to resources, scarcity and prodigality the books were exploring. This highly edited version of the text removes the data Sahlins presents from studies in Arnhem Land and among the !Kung, contemporary hunter-gatherer societies, in order to reveal the underlying polemic—that a principal concern of anthropology should be to critique Western capitalist culture.*

This text was presented as a performative reading at the Geology Museum at Trinity College, Dublin, Ireland and followed by a walk through the city on June 16th & 17th 2011. Organised in association with Second Burial at Le Blanc, *a solo exhibition by Sarah Browne at Project Arts Centre, Dublin.*

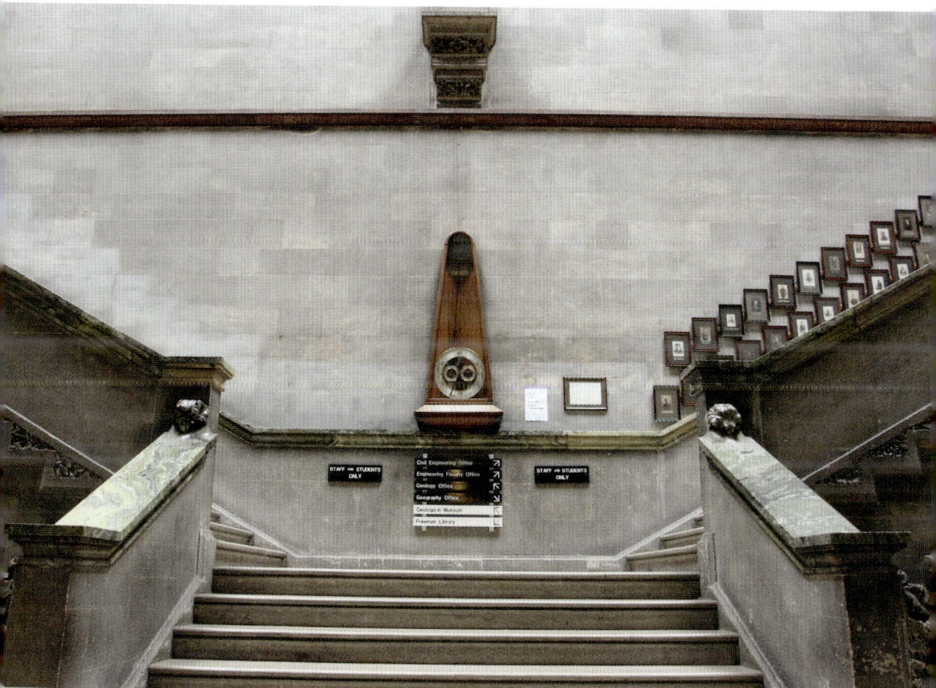
STAFF AND STUDENTS ONLY
Civil Engineering Office
Engineering Faculty Office
Geology Office
Geography Office
Geological Museum
Freeman Library
STAFF AND STUDENTS ONLY

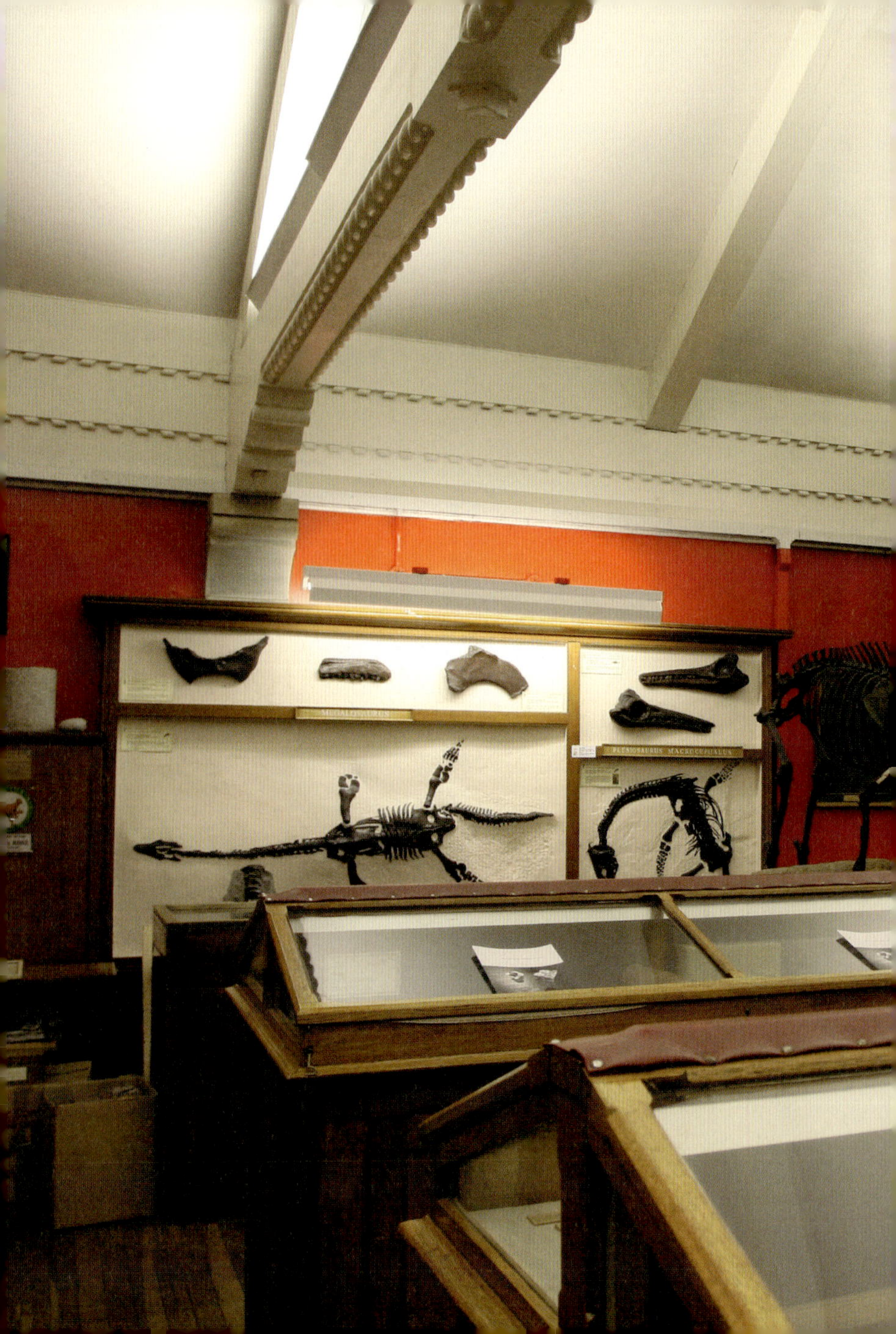

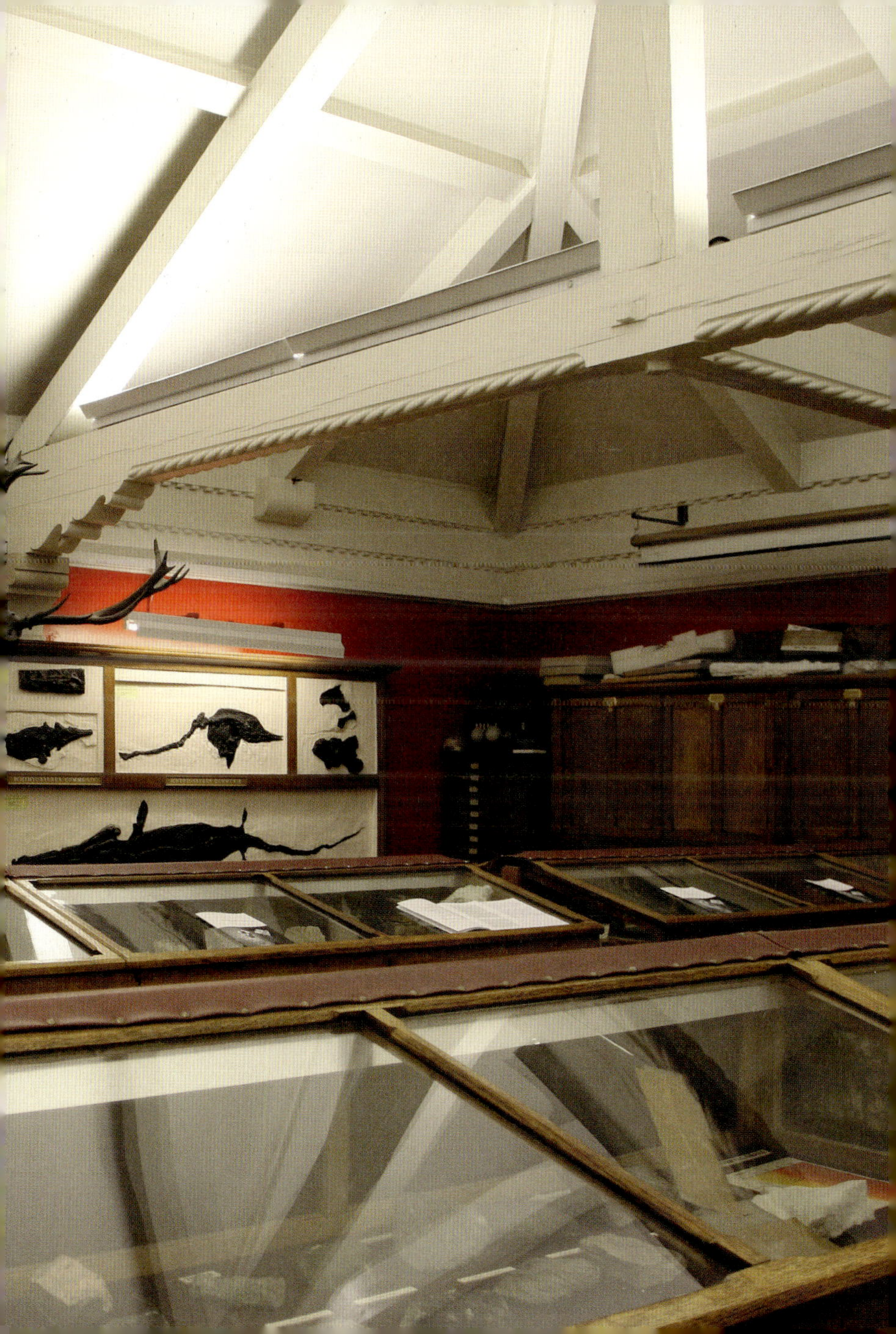

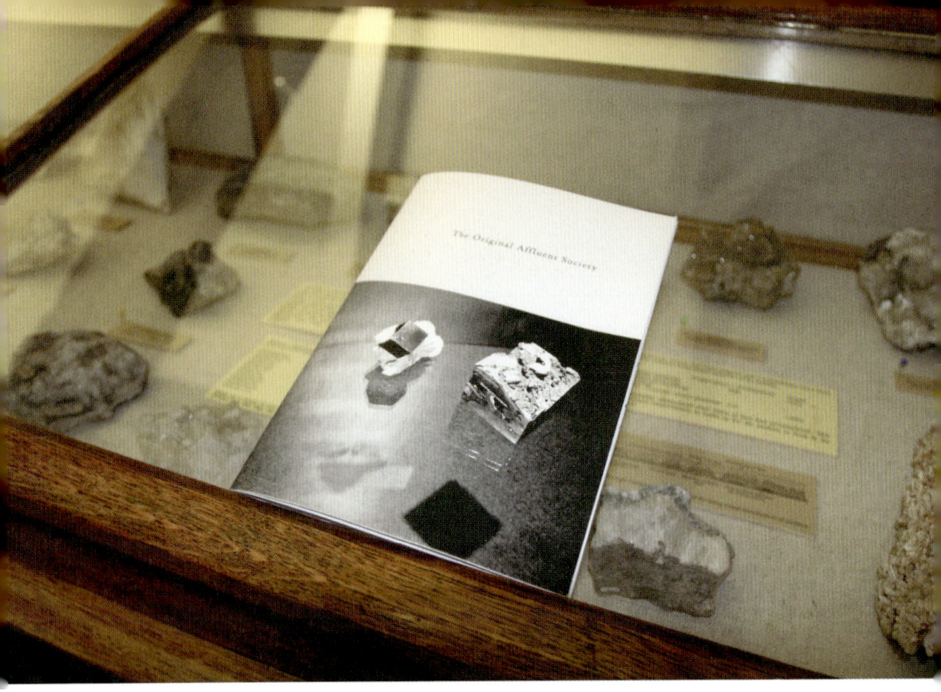
The Original Affluent Society

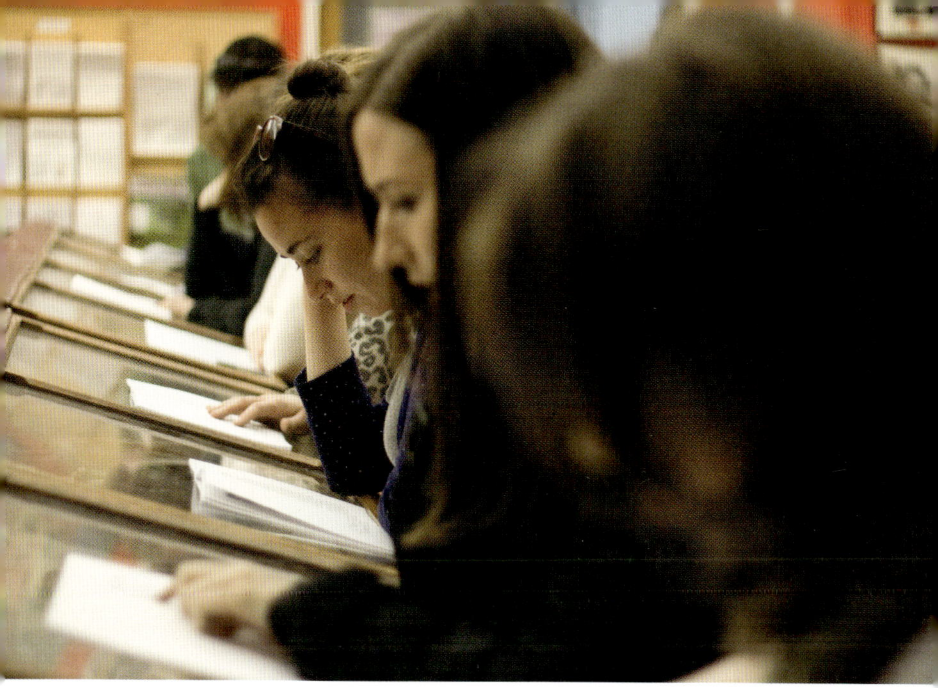

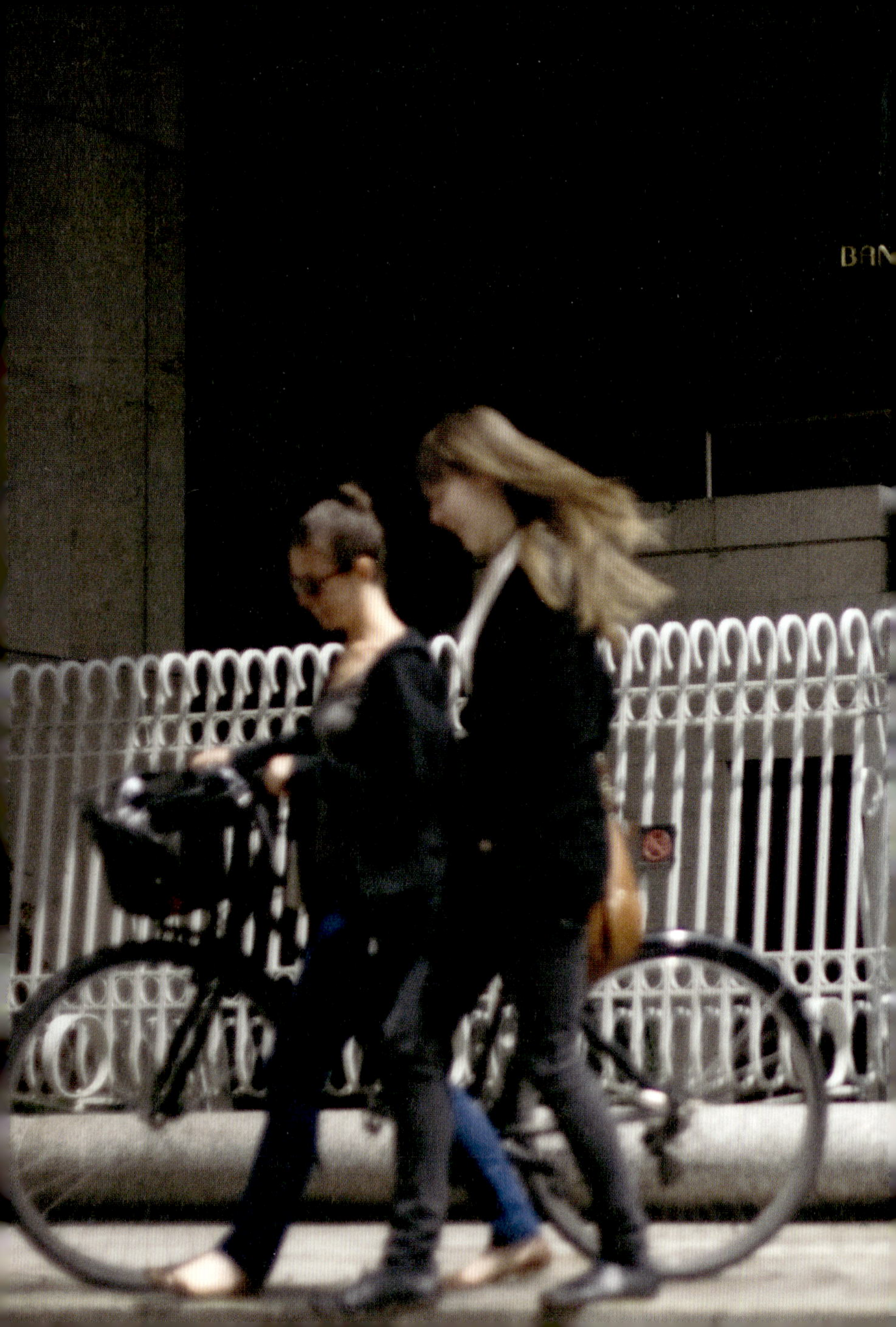

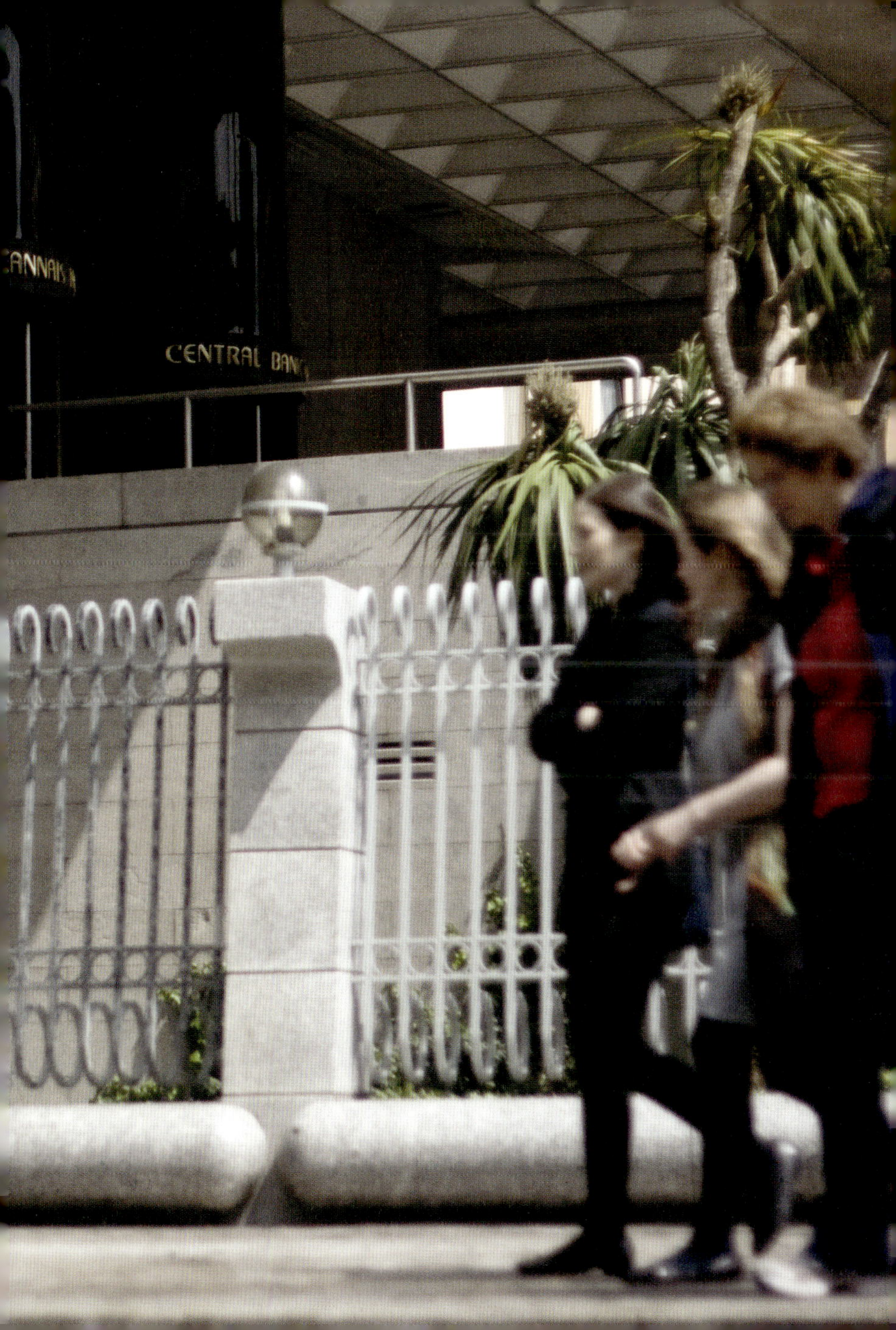
CENTRAL BAN

Models for Central Bank Sculptures, 2011
Cubic crystal of Spanish pyrite, melted and cut decommissioned Irish coinage

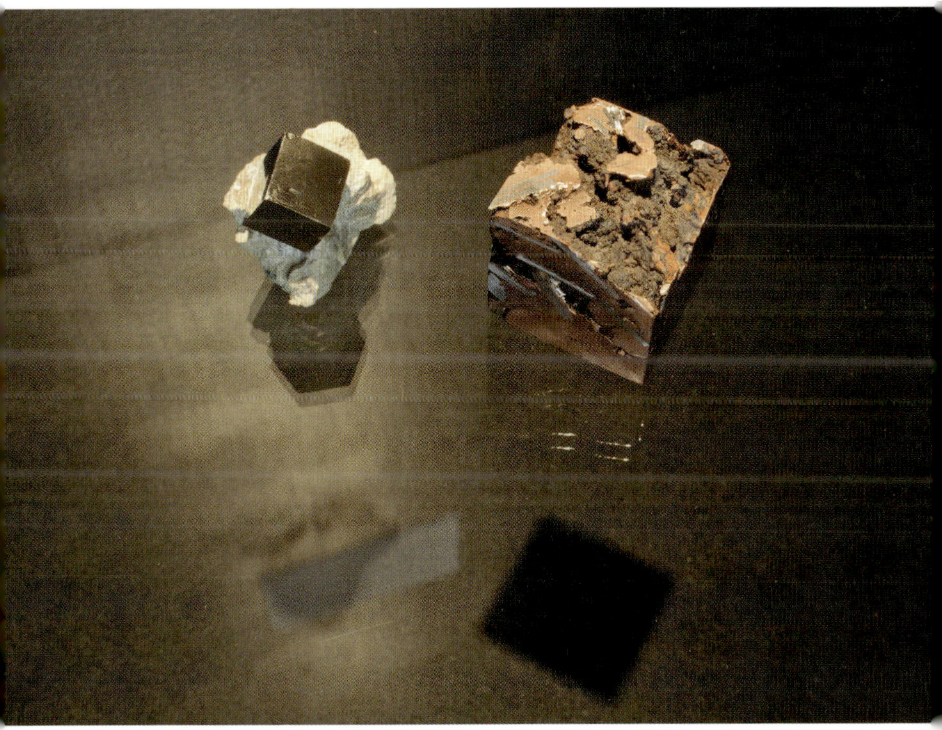

A Model Society, 2007
Respondents to an advertisement by the artist in a Reykjavík newspaper for knitwear models completed a survey relating to life in Iceland, named in 2005 as the happiest country in the world. Icelandic *lopi* sweaters were knitted by the artist for each model, featuring extracts of their responses

35mm slide installation, looped
Dimensions variable (pages 165-175, 182)

Rotten Politics modeled by Arna Bára Karlsdóttir
Expensive modeled by Nalini Gröndal with Bjarni Gröndal
Safe Jobs/ High Taxes modeled by Vesna Jesic Danielsson
Boredom modeled by Vignir Thor Guðmundsson with Iris Arnadóttir and Valey Sol Guðmundsdóttir

Other works in the series: *No War*, *Awesome Daycare*, *Gossip*, *Minority Complex*, *Free Clean Water*, *Long Workhours*, *Exclusive / Isolation*, *The Bank Owns Us*

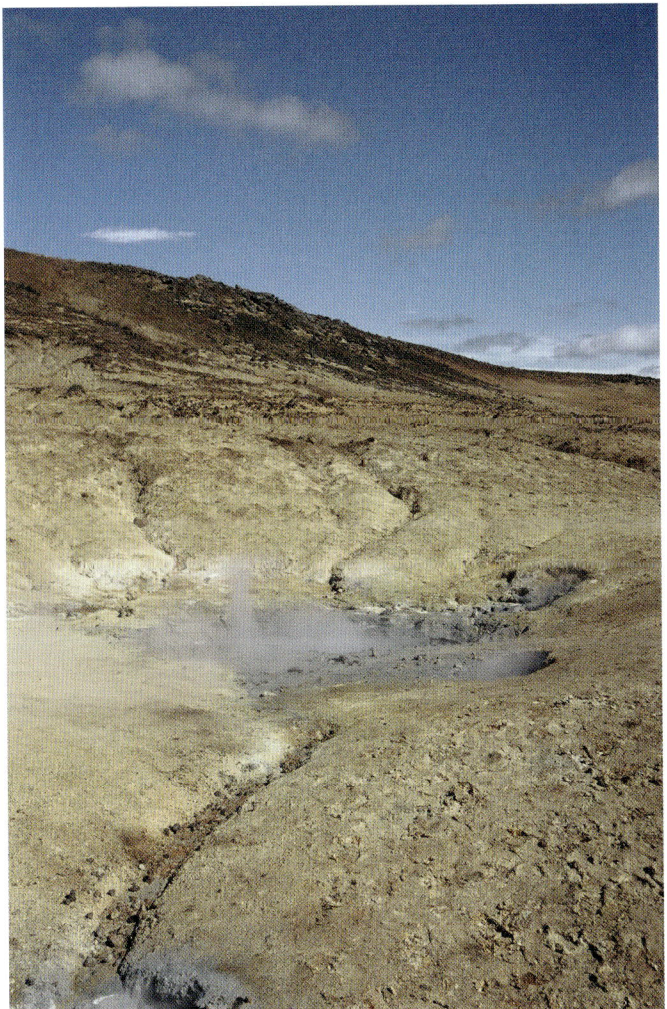

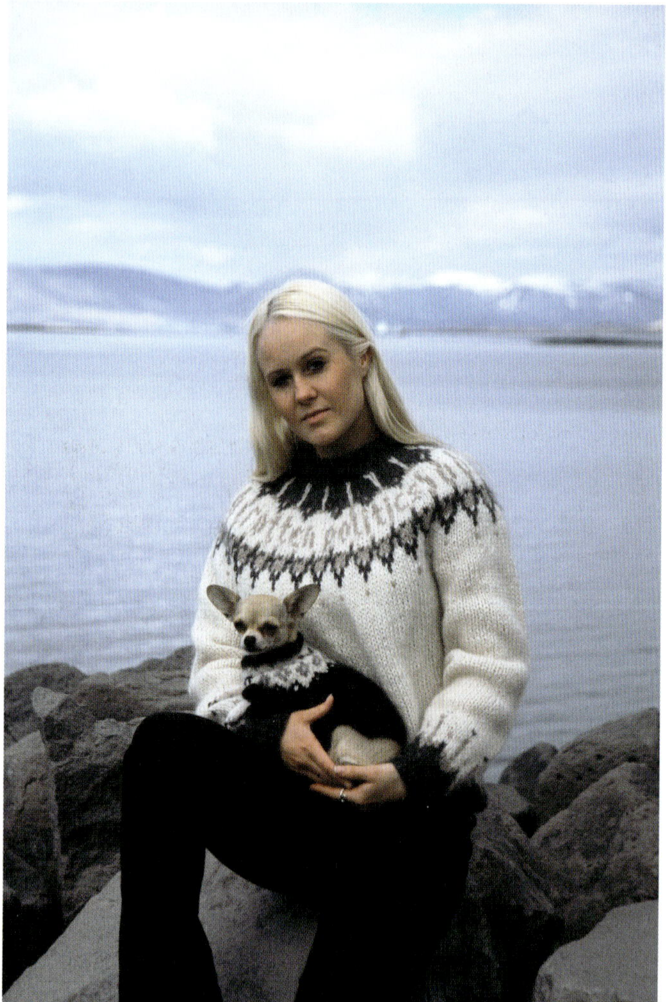
rotten politics

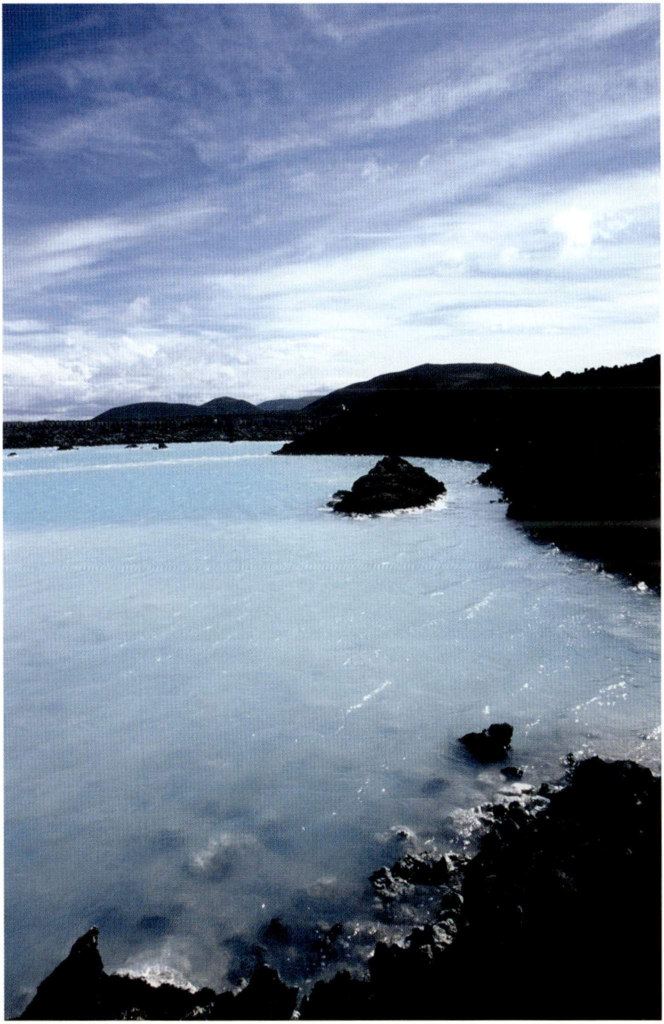

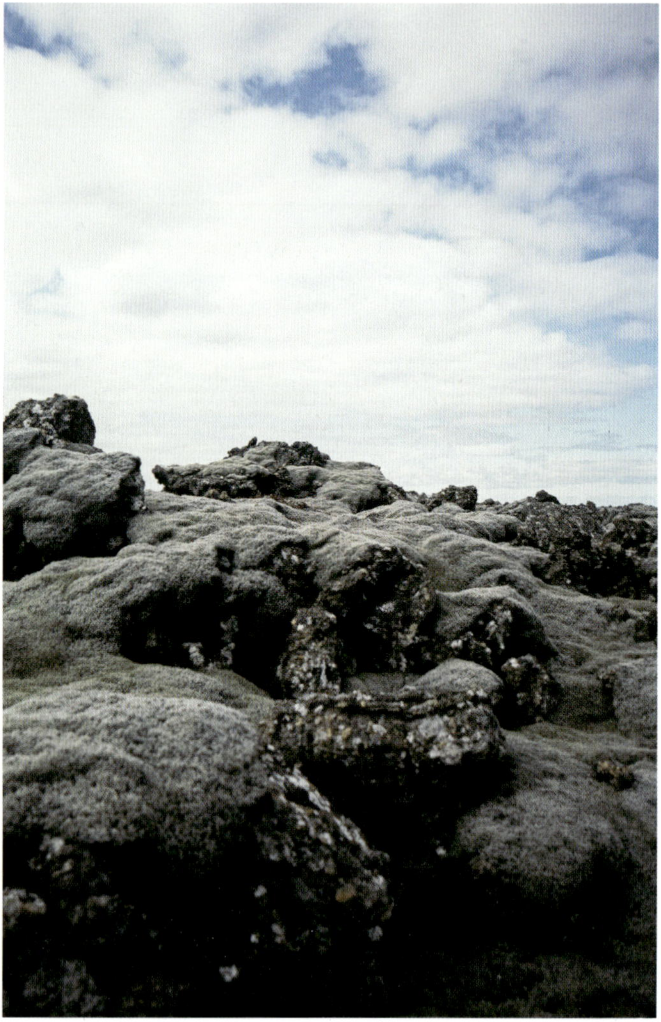

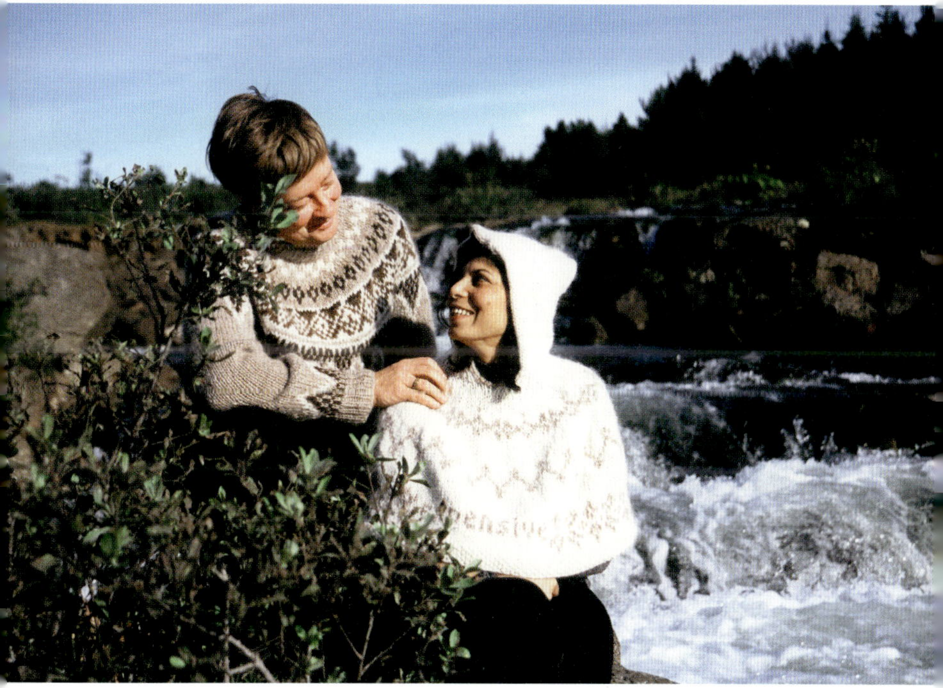

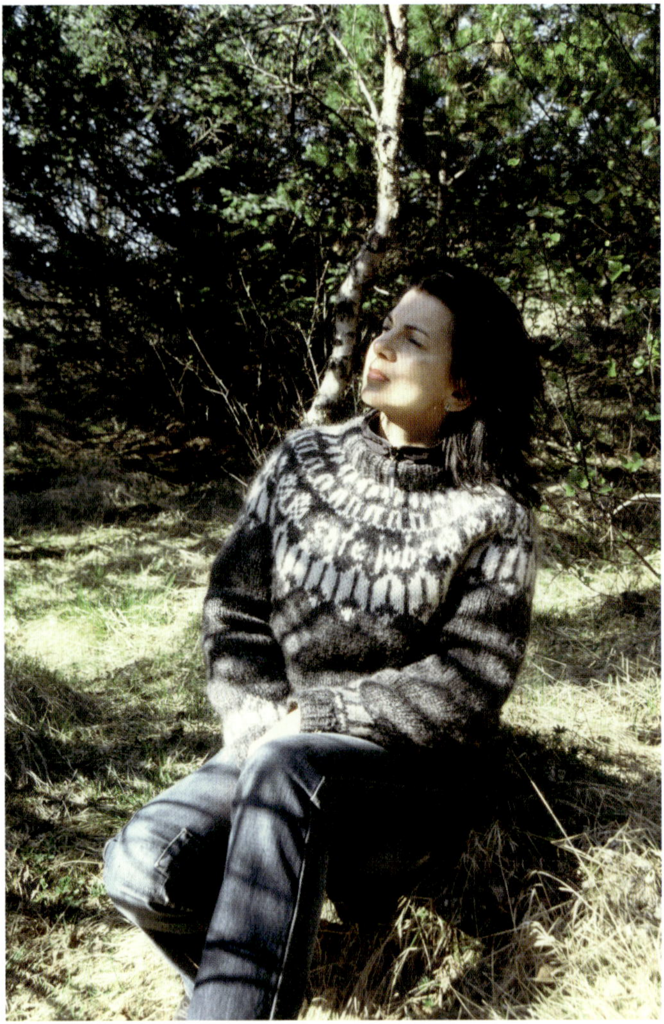

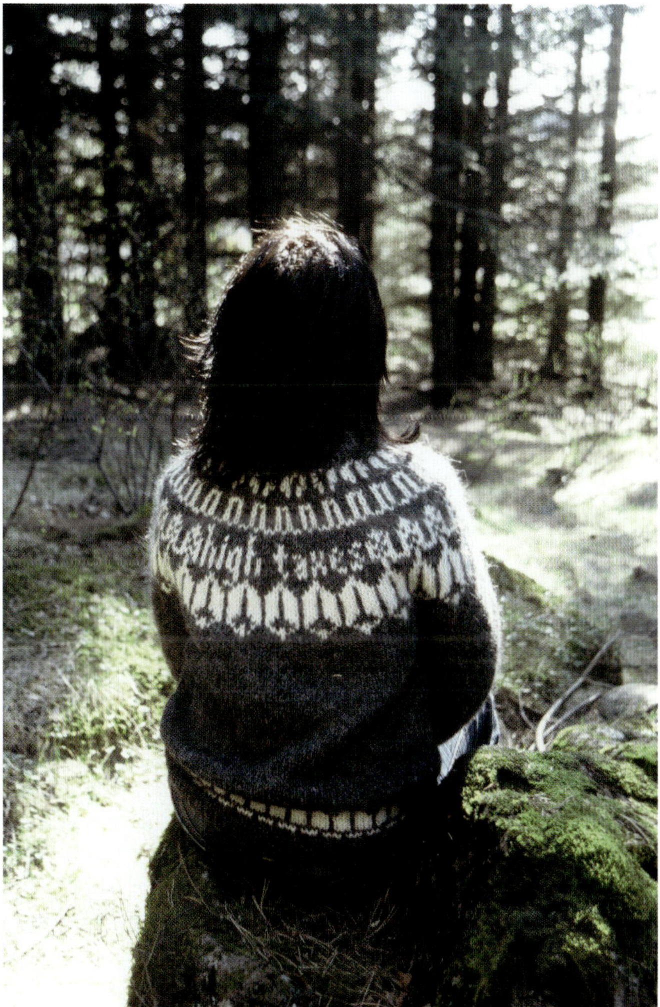

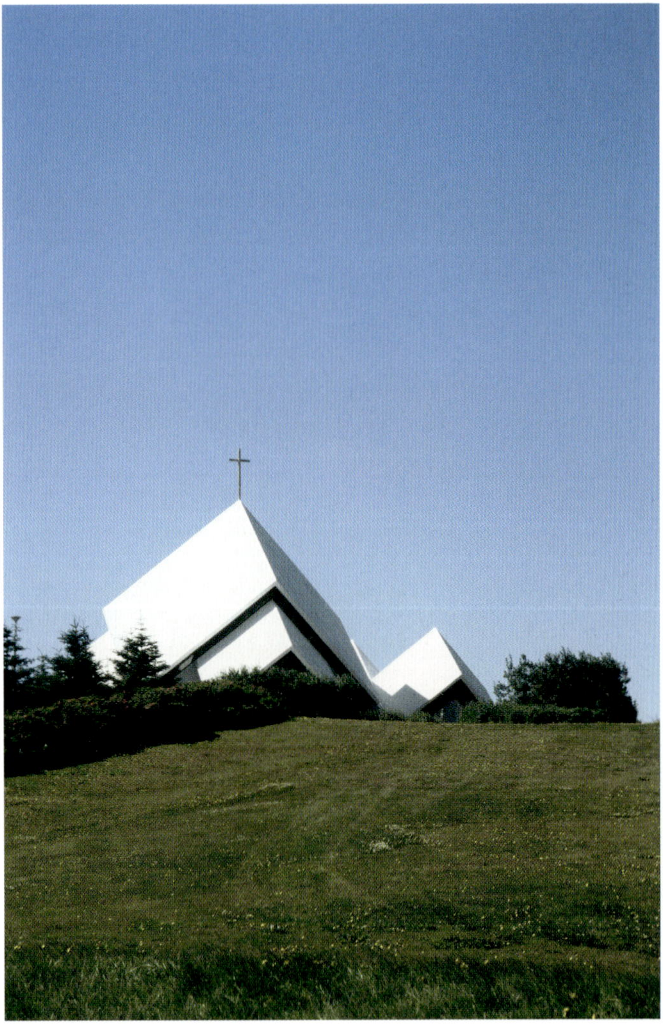

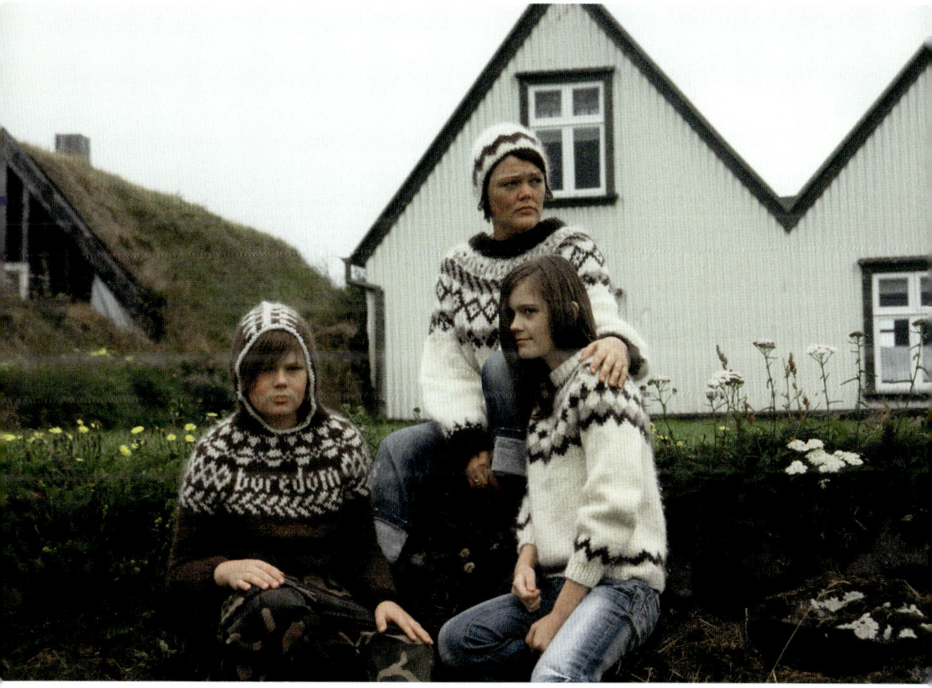
boredom

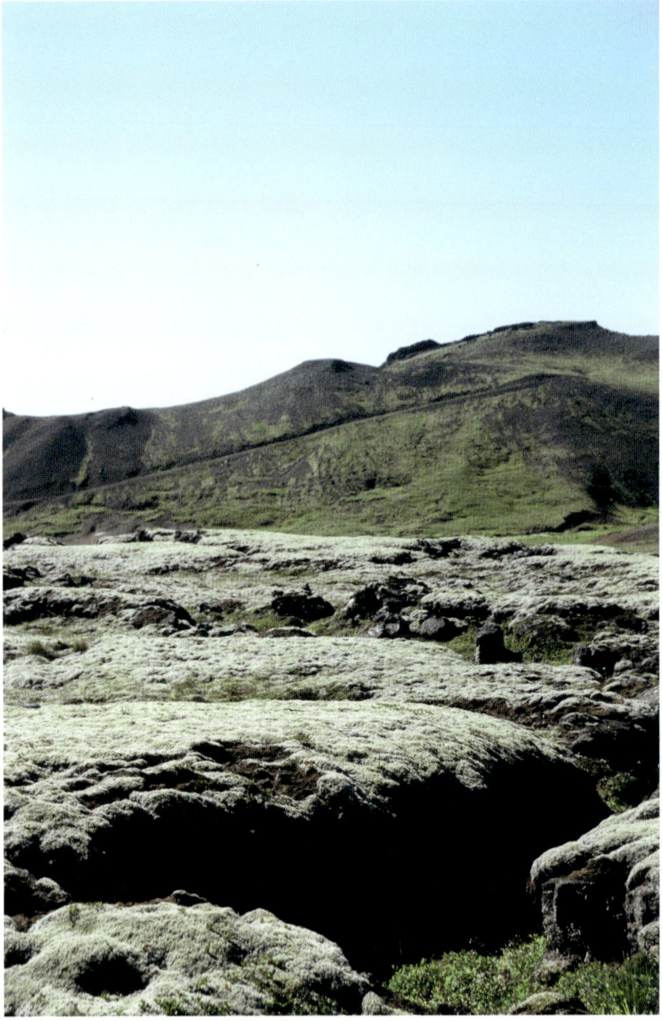

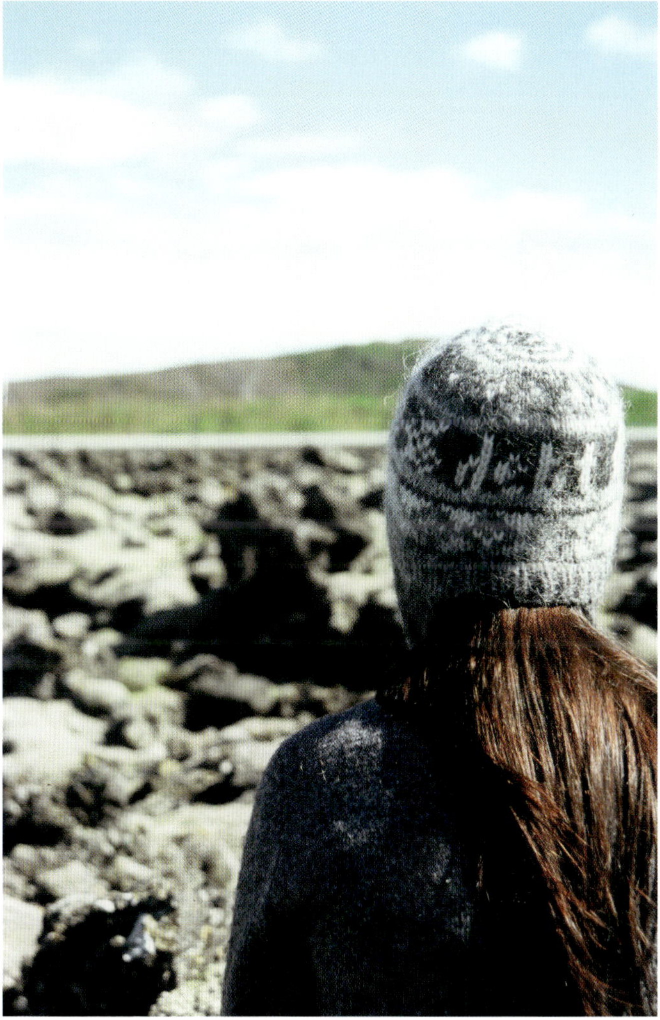

The World Database of Happiness, 2006
Archival print on paper, frame from the National Gallery of Iceland, 480mm x 420mm
Derived from Veenhoven, R., *Happiness in nations, Rank Report 2006-1*
Erasmus University Rotterdam, The Netherlands and www.nationmaster.com

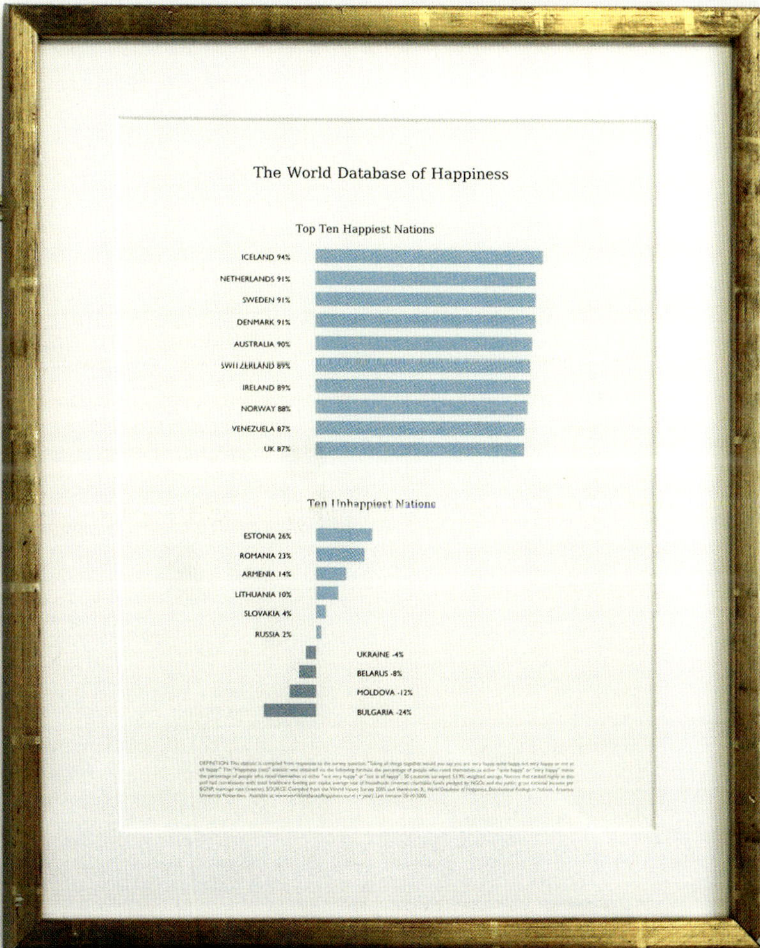
The World Database of Happiness
Top Ten Happiest Nations
ICELAND 94%
NETHERLANDS 91%
SWEDEN 91%
DENMARK 91%
AUSTRALIA 90%
SWITZERLAND 89%
IRELAND 89%
NORWAY 88%
VENEZUELA 87%
UK 87%
Ten Unhappiest Nations
ESTONIA 26%
ROMANIA 23%
ARMENIA 14%
LITHUANIA 10%
SLOVAKIA 4%
RUSSIA 2%
UKRAINE -4%
BELARUS -8%
MOLDOVA -12%
BULGARIA -24%

Sarah Browne's art practice explores our understanding of 'the economy' as the dominant metaphor for contemporary social and political relations. She is concerned with forms of non-market exchange such as gift economies, subsistence, subsidies and poaching, which become both the subject and operation of the work. Flexible in form, the work is often disguised or produced in non-art contexts, and tends to create a temporary community for itself that is invested in its production and circulation. The gallery space, animated with peculiar and somewhat primitive technologies of communication, is then used as a channel for the research and knowledge produced, and a point of connection that draws together places such as Leitrim (rural Ireland), Vaasa (Swedish-speaking Finland) and Le Blanc (pastoral France). Invoking a variety of inventive and problematic documentary strategies, this is an affective geography of desired alternatives that images and describes improbable, but actually existing narratives. As a whole this body of work suggests an acknowledgement of emotional investment in political discourse, and the necessary role of desire in developing new forms of economic and social imagination.

Recent exhibitions include *To Have / To Own*, Kunsti Art Museum, Vaasa, Finland, (2011), *Unto This Last*, Raven Row, London, and *Minimalism and Applied II*, Daimler Contemporary, Berlin (both 2010). In 2009 she co-represented Ireland at the 53rd Venice Biennale with Gareth Kennedy and Kennedy Browne. Recent artist publications, in addition to the versions of works reproduced here, include *From Margin to Margin (Looking for Eileen)* and *Lebensreform in Leitrim* (both 2010). She is currently resident at Firestation Artist Studios, Dublin, and lectures at IADT Dun Laoghaire and the National College of Art and Design, Dublin. www.sarahbrowne.info

Tessa Giblin (1978, New Zealand) is Curator of Visual Arts at Project Arts Centre and was Seminar leader for Curatorial Studies on IADT's Masters in Visual Arts Practices (MAVIS) 2007-09. At Project Arts Centre she has produced solo exhibitions including Clemens von Wedemeyer, Jesse Jones, Lonnie van Brummelen & Siebren de Haan, Aurélien Froment, Geoffrey Farmer & Jeremy Millar and Ceal Floyer, and group exhibitions including *The Prehistory of the Crisis 1&2, Nonknowledge, The Flight of the Dodo, King Rat, Blackboxing,* and *Exhibitions.* She came to Dublin from Amsterdam where she was Head of Exhibitions at Smart Project Space, following the Curatorial Training Program at de Apple in 2005-06. Previously she was Assistant Curator at ARTSPACE, Auckland, and initiated the project space Gridlocked and gallery Fresh, in Christchurch, New Zealand.

Chris Lee is a freelance graphic designer from Toronto, Canada and currently based in The Netherlands where he graduated from the graphic design master's program at the Sandberg Institute (Amsterdam). Chris' recent writing and work have been focused on an exploration of currency towards expanding graphic design's field of concerns to include its relationship to the operation of violence and legitimacy.

Jeremy Millar is an artist living in Whitstable, and tutor in art criticism at the Royal College of Art, London. Recent solo exhibitions include *Mondegreen*, (with Geoffrey Farmer), Project Arts Centre, Dublin (2011); *Resemblances, Sympathies, and Other Acts*, CCA, Glasgow (2011); *Amongst Others*, Plymouth Arts Centre (2010); *As Witkiewicz*, Krakow Ethnographic Museum (2010); Ikon Gallery, Birmingham (2009); and *Given*, National Maritime Museum, London (2009). Recent group exhibitions include *Mystics or Rationalists?*, Ingleby Gallery, Edinburgh (2011); *Never the Same River (Possible Futures, Probable Pasts)*, Camden Art Centre (2010); *Cage Mix*, Baltic, Gateshead (2010); and *The Dark Monarch*, Tate St. Ives (2009). He has written for numerous publications, and his most recent book is *The Way Things Go* (Afterall Books, 2007). He is currently associate research artist at Kettle's Yard, Cambridge.

Marshall Sahlins was born December 27, 1930, Chicago, Illinois and is a prominent American anthropologist. He received both Bachelors and Masters degrees at the University of Michigan where he studied with Leslie White, and earned his Ph.D. at Columbia University in 1954 where his main intellectual influences included Karl Polanyi and Julian Steward. He returned to teach at the University of Michigan and in the 1960s became politically active, protesting against the Vietnam War. In 1968, he signed the 'Writers and Editors War Tax Protest' pledge, vowing to refuse tax payments in protest against the Vietnam War. In the late 1960s he also spent two years in Paris, where he was exposed to French intellectual life (and particularly the work of Claude Lévi-Strauss) and the student protests of May 1968. In 1973 he moved to the University of Chicago, where he is today the Charles F. Grey Distinguished Service Professor of Anthropology Emeritus.

Published on the occasion of:

Sarah Browne

Second Burial at Le Blanc
Project Arts Centre, Dublin
May 6 – June 25, 2011
Curated by Tessa Giblin

How to Use Fool's Gold
Ikon Gallery, Birmingham
February 15 – April 22, 2012
Curated by Tyler Cann
Assisted by Jenine McGaughran

How to Use Fool's Gold
Contemporary Art Gallery, Vancouver
July 13 – September 2, 2012
Curated by Nigel Prince

ISBN 978-1-904864-75-2

Edited by Nigel Prince
Texts by Tessa Giblin, Jeremy Millar
Designed by Peter Maybury
Printed by MM Artbook printing & repro

'The Original Affluent Society' by Marshall Sahlins first appeared in *Stone Age Economics* (Routledge, 1972) and is reproduced here with kind permission of the author and publisher

The original version of 'Alternative Currencies' was published and edited by InCubate for their Pilot Series (Chicago, 2010) and by Metahaven in *The Copyist* for Van Abbemuseum (Eindhoven, 2010). The revised version here with kind permission of the author Chris Lee and publishers

All photos by Sarah Browne except

Eva Herzog (pages 47, 137)
courtesy Raven Row, London

Denis Mortell (pages 48, 54-55, 56-57, 163)

Ros Kavanagh (pages 63, 69)

Hans-Georg Gaul (page 77)
Courtesy Daimler Art Collection, Berlin/Stuttgart

Damien McGlynn (pages 159, 160-61)

Project Press – Project Arts Centre
39 East Essex Street, Temple Bar,
Dublin 2, Ireland
T: +353 1 881 9613
F: +353 1 679 2310
www.projectartscentre.ie

Ikon Gallery
1 Oozells Square, Brindleyplace,
Birmingham, B1 2HS, UK
T: +44 121 248 0708
F: +44 121 248 0709
www.ikon-gallery.co.uk
Registered charity no: 528892

Contemporary Art Gallery
555 Nelson Street, Vancouver,
British Columbia, V6B 6R5, Canada
T: +1 604 681 2700
F: +1 604 683 2710
www.contemporaryartgallery.ca

Distributed by Cornerhouse Publications
70 Oxford Street, Manchester, M1 5NH, UK
publications@cornerhouse.org
T: +44 161 200 1503
F: +44 161 200 1504

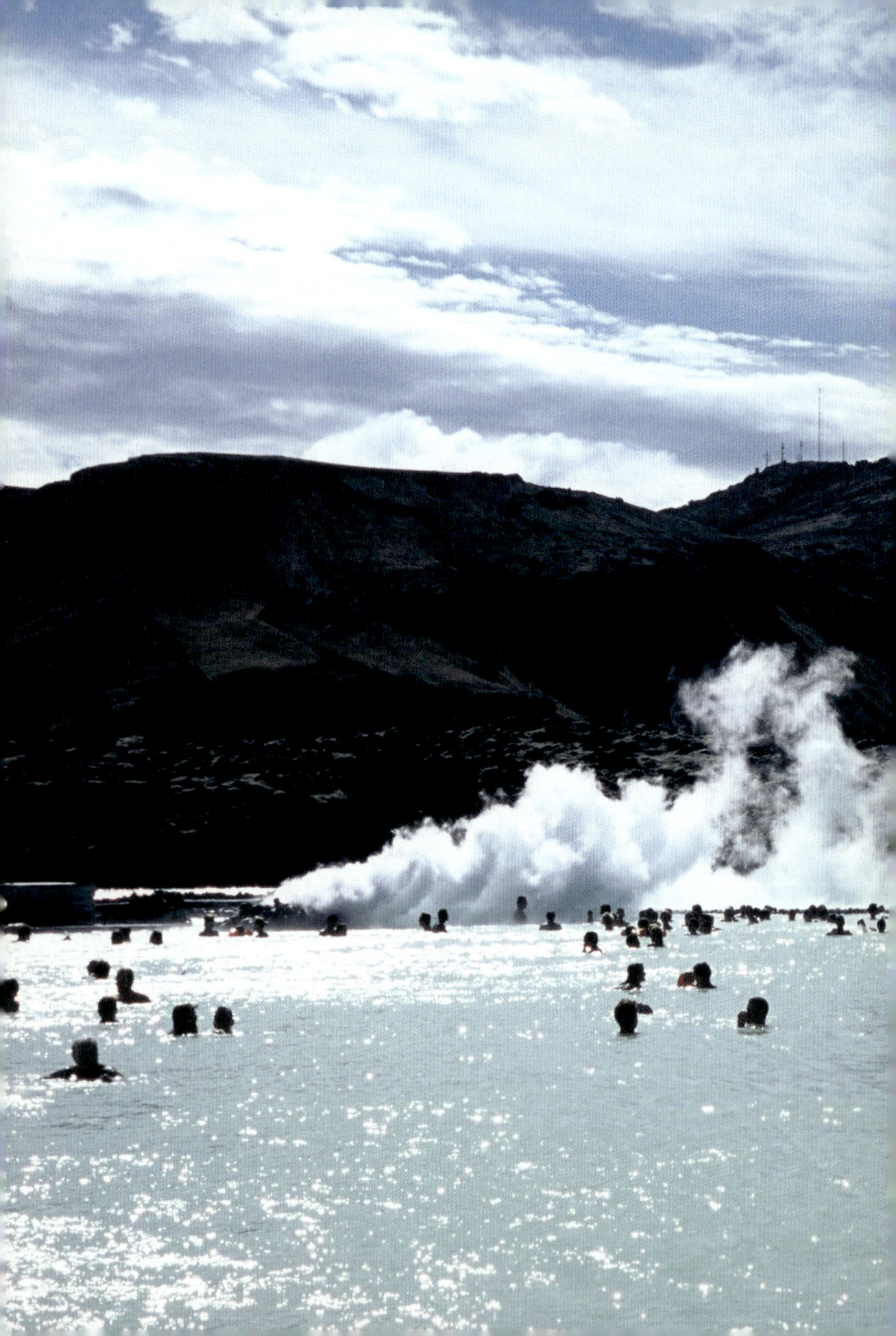

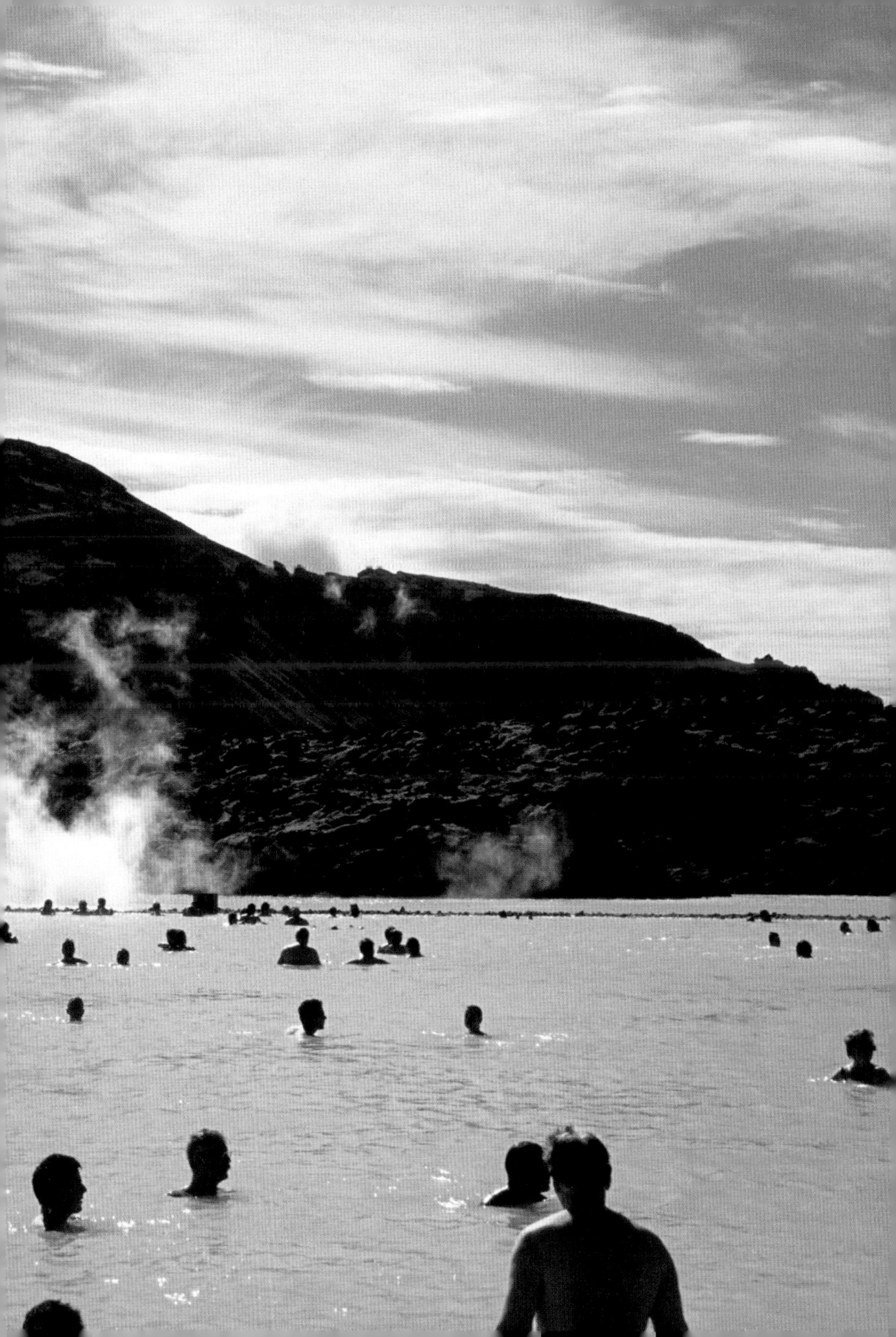

The exhibition at Project Arts Centre is supported by The Arts Council / An Chomhairle Ealaíon and Dublin City Council

The exhibition at Ikon and Contemporary Art Gallery is supported by Culture Ireland

The film *Second Burial at Le Blanc* and accompanying publication *On Hoarding, Accumulating and Gifting* (2011) were supported by a Project Award from The Arts Council / An Chomhairle Ealaíon and produced as a joint commission between Project Arts Centre, Ikon Gallery and the Contemporary Art Gallery on the occasion of the exhibition in Dublin. A second newspaper, *On Excess, Acceleration and Expenditure* (2012) was published to coincide with the exhibition in Birmingham

The artist wishes to thank all who have shared and supported the development of the work presented here. Special thanks to Liam and Mary Browne, Gareth Kennedy, Jesse Jones, Maeve Connolly, Fearghus Ó Conchúir, Linda Doyle and Geoffrey Roberts

Project Arts Centre is supported by The Arts Council / An Chomhairle Ealaíon and Dublin City Council

Ikon gratefully acknowledges financial assistance from Arts Council England and Birmingham City Council

The Contemporary Art Gallery is financially supported by the Canada Council for the Arts, the City of Vancouver and the Province of BC through the BC Arts Council and the BC Gaming Policy and Enforcement Branch. We are also grateful for the support of Vancouver Foundation and our members, donors, and volunteers

project arts centre
the arts council an chomhairle ealaíon — funding the arts — artscouncil.ie
Dublin City Baile Átha Cliath
Culture Ireland Cultúr Éireann

IKON
Birmingham City Council
Arts Council England — Supported by ARTS COUNCIL ENGLAND

CAG
British Columbia The Best Place on Earth
City of Vancouver
British Columbia Arts Council An agency of the Province of British Columbia
Canada Council for the Arts Conseil des Arts du Canada